WINNING GOALS

MAKING
YOUR DREAMS REAL

Sound Wisdom
P.O. Box 310
Shippensburg, PA 17257-0310

Reach us on the Internet: www.soundwisdom.com.

ISBN 13 TP: 978-0-7684-1089-1
ISBN 13 Ebook: 978-0-7684-1092-1

Cover design by Eileen Rockwell

For Worldwide Distribution, Printed in the U.S.A.
1 2 3 4 5 6 7 8 / 20 19 18 17 16

CONTENTS

THE FAIRYTALE THEORY

Every fairytale starts with "Once upon a time" and ends with "And they lived happily ever after." What make these fairytales interesting are the things that happen in between. The crux of the story is in between the start and the end. In our case, we call that part *life*.

What if you had the power to script your own fairytale? You would certainly want it to end on "And I lived happily ever after," right? In order to get from "Once upon a time" to the "happily ever after," you will have to go through *life*. That is the real challenge.

The most interesting aspect of writing your own script is that you can choose the where, why, when, with whom, and how. Let's remove the "if" from "what if." You have to believe that you have the power to write your own fairytale. All you need is the desire to do so. Once you have that desire, set goals, back those up with actions, and you are all set to script the best story ever. Get...Set...Goals!

WHAT CAN THIS BOOK GIVE YOU?

The power of leading a goal-oriented life—that's the promise this book holds. It will take you on a journey where you will be able to visualize the life that you always wanted to live.

Get acquainted with and practice the techniques provided in this book and you will see that you can widen your horizons and view life with a renewed spirit and a positive attitude. The techniques, methods, and exercises provided in this book will help you live your dream.

The book has nine chapters that will teach you the value of goals and ways and means to achieve them. The chapters are supported by interesting stories that will change your perception of life.

The book delves into the psychology and subconscious part of goals and the right approach to overcome barriers. The additional section at the end presents you with a hundred ways to live that can take you to your goals and ensure that you stay there.

HOW TO USE THIS BOOK

Throughout this book, you will live your life over and over again. You will revisit your past, think about the present, and dream about the future. The techniques, stories, and exercises in the book will help you analyze your life and develop a game plan. This will take you to your ultimate goal and a balanced life.

Try out the exercises in the book, make notes along the way, and refer to them whenever a similar point comes up in the course. This is not a one-time journey; you can revisit this book whenever you want. Reading it once will definitely help you reach your goal; reading it again and again will make sure that you do not drift away from it.

Remember that every time you read this book, you will be at a different stage of your life. At each point, this book will help you regain your focus on the renewed goals and unlock the hidden passageways to your goals.

So go ahead, use this book to achieve your goals and live your dream. When you do, make sure you share this wisdom with your loved ones.

Do not wait...go for your *goals!*

Chapter 1

THE JOURNEY BEGINS

ADVENTURES AND MAPS

Imagine embarking on an adventurous journey to a place where you have always wanted to go. It can be an island with azure water, white sandy beaches, coconut trees and a beautiful sunset; tranquil, snow-clad mountains in the midst of nowhere; or perhaps a forest reserve with all sorts of flora and fauna; maybe even a bustling city with large malls offering great discounts. Think of your dream destination and start preparing for the journey.

Once you have zeroed in on a destination, you will naturally start figuring out everything you need to get going. You will plan the bookings and the reservations, figure out ways and means to reach there, and search for the best route possible. You have a roadmap in place, and you try to stick to it to reach your destination.

A few adventurous people will say that they do not need a map to go anywhere. They can reach their dream destination without the help of a map. After all, what is life without its adventures, they might say. If you belong to that category, let's say you put yourself in the driver's seat and venture out toward your destination.

You are cruising along the road listening to your favorite track on the radio. Suddenly, it gets a little overcast and foggy. Being a very strong person, you continue driving. As you go along, you see no one on the highway. The sky is turning red and the heat is getting to you. You are sweating profusely, breathing heavily, and cannot see a thing except the dark red sky. Nervousness sinks in and anxiety drives you crazy. You hit a dead end and look around, but there is no one and nowhere to go. You are lost.

That's when an old man knocks on your window and tells you that you took a wrong turn and lends you a map. Now, you feel secure and confident about yourself and about reaching your destination. Now, you have a roadmap in place and you follow it. That is when you realize that there is a fine line between being adventurous and being stupid.

So, if you cannot embark on a journey without a map or a set destination, how can you embark on the journey of your life without one? The map is an analogy for your *goals*. Once you have your goals in place, you can cruise confidently along the journey called *life*.

MOUNTAIN MAN

Soccer is an engaging game; it is action-packed and unpredictable. Any team can win or lose from any position;

that's what makes it exciting. Twenty-two players constantly run after a ball with the purpose of either scoring a goal or defending a goal. Take the goal out of the picture and they are a bunch of twenty-two players running around the ball without any sense of purpose. The goal is their purpose.

Similarly, your goals are the purpose of your life. It doesn't have to be the ultimate goal. It can be smaller goals leading up to the big one. A goal can be as small as waking up at 6 a.m. or as big as being the owner of a billion-dollar enterprise. The magnitude of your goal depends upon you.

People say that love can move mountains. A man in Bihar, India proved this by carving through a mountain with a chisel and a hammer—for love. Dashrath Manjhi, affectionately called, "The Mountain Man," single-handedly carved out a 360-foot long, 25-foot high, and 30-foot wide road through a mountain. Dashrath was an ordinary, landless farmer who lived in the Gehlaur area near Gaya in Bihar, India. The prominent mountain in the village isolated the villagers; they had to venture on an arduous and dangerous trek every day just to reach their fields or the market.

On one such perilous trek in 1960, Dashrath's wife, Phalguni Devi, suffered a severe injury on the treacherous mountain road. As medical help could not be reached in time, she passed away. Sparked by the love for his wife and the motive that no one else should suffer the same fate, he decided to make a passage through the mountain all by himself. He set his goal to carve through the mountain and that became the purpose of his life. Initially people laughed at him, but he never lost his purpose. He carved the mountain inch by inch, often singing his way through. After a period, the villagers started providing him food and water in order to help him in his pursuit.

He worked relentlessly day and night through the scorching heat and the chilly winters to defeat the mountain. After twenty-two years of determination and hard work, he hammered the mountain the final time in 1982. Dashrath Manjhi achieved his goal of carving a road out of a mountain! He fought nature and the government and reduced the distance between the Atri and Wazirganj blocks of Gaya district from 75 kilometers to just 1 kilometer!

If man can carve through a mountain with nothing but a hammer and chisel, he can do anything. You have the power to achieve whatever you want in life.

If you do not know your destination, how can you expect to get there?

Before that, you need to know what you want to achieve in order to get there. If you do not know your destination, how can you expect to get there? Identify your goals and purpose in life and work relentlessly; you can chisel through the mountain too.

LIKE MONKEYS AND MEN

Goals are evolutionary in nature. Just like life evolved on the earth from a single cell, goals evolve throughout a person's life.

We wouldn't have evolved if we hadn't been ambitious. The hunger for more has brought us from leading life in the caves to a sophisticated life; it has the potential to take us to faraway places in the future. Evolutions and revolutions have taken place because of goals.

Goals evolve at each stage of life. A toddler's goal might be to stay nourished and be cared for; a teenager's goal might be to excel in her chosen field of study; a newly married person might aspire for a good professional and personal life. A new mom might dream to provide for her child so it wants nothing more, and an elder's goal might be to see her children and grandchildren prospering.

The evolutionary nature of goals also means that the person setting the goals for you changes. As a kid, your parents set your goals. They teach you everything they know. They imbue in you certain values and principles that help you achieve your goals.

As you grow up, your teachers set your goals. The human mind absorbs the most when it is growing. Thus, teachers play a crucial part not only in setting your goals at that stage of life but also in affecting your thought process, which eventually orients you toward your goals. Teachers consciously and subconsciously teach you ways to achieve your goals. Your learning curve is therefore aligned toward success from a young age.

As an adult, you become responsible and accountable. That is when the onus of setting goals falls entirely on your shoulders. More than your strengths and abilities, it is the choices that you make to channel them that define you. If you do not set goals for yourself, someone else will do it for you to accomplish their goals. You will lose your purpose and serve someone else's purpose.

When you start your own family, you have the dual role of pursuing your goals as well as setting goals for your children. You have to be in command to lead your life toward a goal. At every evolutionary stage, you have the choice either to evolve or dissolve. The decision, as always, lies with you.

THE MARATHONER'S WISDOM

In the Tokyo International Marathon in 1984, a Japanese marathoner, Yamada, unexpectedly won the world championship. At a press conference, the reporters asked him the reason for his success. He replied that he had used wisdom to stay on the right track and defeat the opponents. The reporters were bewildered by his answer, as marathon running is a sport that is dominated by physical endurance and strength. Wisdom was not the answer they had expected.

Two years later, Yamada won the world championship again in the Italian International Marathon. The reporters asked him the same question. He repeated that he had used wisdom to stay on the right track and defeat the opponent.

The reporters were confused yet again; they did not understand the connection between wisdom and running a race.

The reporters, along with the rest of the world, had to wait for a while to learn about Yamada's wisdom. Ten years later, Yamada's answer was decoded from his autobiography where he explained what he meant by wisdom.

Before every race, he would travel the whole track and scrutinize it carefully. He would scout the locality and make notes about the adjoining landmarks like "the big tree," "the bank," "the red-colored house," etc. that enabled him to break the race into small checkpoints.

He would make strategies accordingly and outsmart the opponent by managing his speed depending on the checkpoints. His wisdom prompted him to break the major goal of winning the race into smaller goals of reaching checkpoints swiftly. The checkpoints aligned him toward his ultimate goal and kept him on track to win the race.

Goals are like the GPS in your car. They help you reach your destination and warn you if you deviate from your path.

Whether your objective is to win a race or to achieve professional success, goals will help you be on the right track. Goals act like the Global Positioning System (GPS) in your car. They help you reach your destination and warn you if you deviate from your path.

Your goals will guide you toward your dreams. Life's challenges force us to deviate from our path, but our goals guide us and remind us to stick to the right path.

DREAM MERCHANT

Each and every one of us has a dream merchant inside. This dream merchant fuels our aspirations and desires. It feeds on whatever we think and ought to become, resonates it, and builds an illusion. The dream merchant is a double-edged sword and excels in the art of escapism. We have to be aware of it to grasp our reality and not fall prey to its illusions.

The dream merchant's magic can be channeled effectively if we convert those dreams into goals. This conversion will transmit the power from the dreams into goals and allow us to lift the curtain over illusions to visualize reality. As mentioned earlier, your goals will guide you toward the ultimate goal of achieving your dreams.

There is a huge difference between goals and dreams. Let's unravel the mystery of the dream merchant and its illusions by understanding the difference between dreams and goals.

Lights. Camera. Action!

Dreams do not require any actions. You can dream about anything and everything. However, in order to achieve a goal, we have to work toward it.

Tick Toc

Dreams do not have a deadline. Goals need to be accomplished by a certain time or they become obsolete. That is not the case with dreams; one can keep on dreaming for eternity.

Do You Invest?

Dreams do not require any sort of investment. You can dream for free. That is not the case with goals. You have to invest your time, money, and energy in pursuit of your goals until you achieve them.

Goals give a sense of direction to your dreams.

What's Your Score?

Dreaming is an illusion; it does not result in anything. Achieving goals leads to results.

Reality Check

Dreams are in fantasy world. Goals remind you about reality. They shake you and wake you up from the alluring fantasy world.

You Want It to End

Goals end; dreams do not. Goals end and give rise to other goals to keep you motivated, but dreaming is an unending process.

Eyes on the Prize

Dreams do not require focus. Goals require a focused approach. You have to stick to your goals to reach the desired outcome.

No Free Lunch

Dreaming is very easy; it does not require any hard work. Achieving goals requires an immense amount of hard work.

S.O.L.I.D

Dreams are intangible, but goals are well defined. Dreams have the ability to inspire you, but goals have the power to channel that inspiration into something tangible.

When you put a timeline on your dreams, they become your goals. Goals give a sense of direction to your dreams. You start taking steps to achieve your goals and convert your dreams into reality.

When you put a timeline on your dreams, they become your goals.

THE GOAL-SETTING NIGHTMARE

Some people are good at setting goals, while some are not. Let's understand what stops people from setting goals and ways to find out how to overcome those barriers.

Many times people find it extremely difficult to set a goal. They have nightmares when they are forced to set a goal. Nevertheless, they find it is easy to set goals for others. When it comes to setting goals for themselves, they seem hesitant and falter in their attempt. The goal-setting nightmare has affected many people mainly because of the following barriers:

The Default Setting

By default, people are negative. They see the downside rather than watching the upside of things. Whenever they gain the courage to set a goal for themselves, negative scenarios creep up in their mind and cripple their self-belief. They start focusing on the negatives rather than the positives.

The best way to overcome such a scenario is to let negativity affect you but only for a while. Let it do its thing, but just when you are about to abandon your goal, think of the positives. The gloom will lift and you will see the light at the end of the tunnel. Remember that all the darkness in the world cannot extinguish the light of a single candle.

The Tiny Thing Called Failure

People are afraid of failure. More than the concept of failure, they fear its consequences. The thought of failing to achieve the goal stops them from setting one. They are of the opinion that with the absence of a goal they will avoid failure.

Failing at a task is not the ultimate failure; failing to try is. Failure teaches us to look at things from a different perspective. It allows us to analyze our strengths and weaknesses in a profound manner. Wear failure like armor to protect yourself from overconfidence.

The Same Ol' Road

People have a limited scope of thinking. They cannot expand the horizons of their mind and think beyond a point. The magnitude of their goals scares them. They are content with small goals and do not expand their scope. They are not content; they are terrified of the efforts demanded by the size of goals.

You cannot explore new avenues if you keep traveling the known road. When people are comfortable with small goals but are afraid of a huge goal, then all they have to do is align small goals toward their ultimate goal. Staring at a huge goal indeed is very scary, but it can be accomplished by breaking it down into small, achievable goals.

The Others Syndrome

Unfortunately, we live in a society where people decide their worth depending on the opinion of others. They fear getting rejected by society for the things they have not even started. The others syndrome pushes you down and doesn't allow you to rise above the clutter.

Everyone is fighting his or her own battle. People have neither the time nor the right to judge you. They may have opinions, but they are not judgements and you do not need to live your life on others' terms and conditions. Rise above what others may think of you and achieve your goals, and then they will start taking notice of your efforts.

Timeless Tomorrow

People have the habit of postponing things. They like to play catch up when they can dictate terms. Many times people have a strong desire to achieve a goal. They back it up with a suitable action plan. When it comes to the execution part, they postpone it to tomorrow.

The funny thing about tomorrow is that it is never going to come today. You need to focus your energies on what you have today and strive hard to achieve your goals without postponing it to the uncertain future.

The "I Cannot" Sickness

Often people doubt their abilities and do not have faith in themselves. They lack the self-esteem that stops them from thinking positively about their goals. They do not have the inspiration or the drive to succeed. They have the necessary arsenal to achieve their goals but lack the conviction to do so.

Lack of conviction can only be overcome by raising your self-esteem. You deserve love and affection. The first step to making people believe in you is to believe in yourself. You have to believe that you are capable of giving your hundred percent to your goal. Do not judge it by success or failure but the effort you have put in to cherish and achieve your goal.

Inside Four Walls

People do not set goals because that is not what they think is important. They have grown up without being oriented toward a goal-based approach. They don't have anyone in their social circle with a defined goal. One cannot blame them for not being able to set a goal because they haven't set one ever.

However, it is never too late to start. For people who have never set goals, it is important to begin with setting smaller goals before graduating to the big league. Change is the only constant, and when you have set goals in place you will notice a positive change in yourself.

Do not be afraid of the goal-setting nightmare; just open your eyes and realize that reality is much scarier if you do not have goals to guide you through it. Life is a journey, and having well-defined goals will ensure that you have a happy journey.

CHAPTER REWIND
CHAPTER REWIND

- Your goals are the purpose of your life.

- If you do not set goals for yourself, someone else will do it for you to accomplish their goals. You will lose your purpose and serve someone else's purpose.

- Learn to tame your dream merchant.

- Remember that all the darkness in the world cannot extinguish the light of a single candle.

- Failing at a task is not the ultimate failure; failing to try is.

- You cannot explore new avenues if you keep travelling the known road.

- The funny thing about tomorrow is that it is never going to come today.

Chapter 2

GOALS AND NEEDS

"Many people have a wrong idea of what constitutes true happiness. It is not attained through self-gratification but through fidelity to a worthy purpose."
—HELEN KELLER

ANTHONY VERSUS TIME

What would happen to your state of mind if you were told that you had a brain tumor and it would kill you in a year's time? Anthony Burgess found himself in a similar position when he was 40 years old. He was diagnosed with a brain tumor and had a one-year deadline to survive. He wanted to leave something behind for his wife, Lynne, after his death. So, he renewed his goals.

Anthony Burgess had never been a professional novelist before, but he knew that he had always had the potential to be one. Now that the universe had set a deadline on his dreams, he rekindled his goal and pursued writing a novel. With the thought of leaving the royalties of the book for his wife, he set to work. He did not know whether his novel would be published or not. His only purpose was to write.

The year was 1960 and the prognosis suggested that Anthony had a winter, spring, and summer to live and he would perish with the fall of the leaf. Chasing his goal, Anthony wrote five and a half novels before his deadline. After the deadline, the leaf fell but he survived, as the tumor had gone into remission. He went on to write over 50 books, 3 symphonies, over 150 musical works, and other literary works! The one-year deadline changed Anthony Burgess's life completely.

Are you waiting for an external force to set a deadline for you? Here is an exercise for you. Imagine what you would do if you had a year to live. Make a list of these things. What next, you ask? Well, start working on the list *now*.

STACK 'EM UP

Renowned psychologist Abraham Maslow suggested that our actions are motivated in order to achieve our needs or goals. His need hierarchy theory states that people are motivated to fulfil basic needs before moving on to other advanced needs.

MASLOW'S PYRAMID

The hierarchy is often represented in the form of a pyramid, called Maslow's pyramid. The bottom levels comprise the basic needs while the top levels consist of more complex needs.

1. *Physiological Needs*

These are the basic needs of food, clothing, shelter, etc. It is important to fulfil these needs for our survival. Only when we fulfil these needs can we move on to satisfy other needs. We have to create a firm base for the pyramid to grow.

2. *Safety and Security Needs*

We need a safe environment for survival. Our goal at this stage is to find ways to survive in the urban jungle. Needs like steady employment, healthcare, safe neighborhood, etc. fall under this category. We have to fulfil them in order to move to the next level.

People are motivated to fulfil basic needs before moving on to other advanced needs.

3. Social Needs

Man is a social animal. We long for love, affection, and belonging. At this stage, our goals are to fulfil our social needs, which range from friendships, family, romantic attachments, etc. People join various groups and communities to fulfil their goal of companionship and acceptance.

4. Esteem Needs

Our self-esteem needs revolve around personal worth, social recognition, and accomplishment. Our goals are centered on fulfilling these needs and raising our self-esteem.

5. Self-Actualization

Our ultimate goal is to reach this level of the pyramid. Self-actualization pertains to self-awareness. At this stage, we are concerned about our personal growth and not perturbed by the opinion of others.

We come across various stages in our life, and at each stage we strive to achieve specific goals. If we start thinking of all the goals at a particular time, it will result in utter chaos. The hierarchy of goals helps us concentrate on one particular goal at a time.

THE HARVARD EXPERIMENT

In the year 1979, students of the Harvard MBA program were asked to set clearly defined written goals for their future and make plans to accomplish them. Only 3 percent of the students had been able to list their goals and plans, while 13 percent of the students had mentioned their goals but could not plan their course to achieve them. Eighty-four percent of the students had not mentioned their goals at all.

Ten years later, the same batch of students were interviewed again, and the findings of the study were as follows. The 13 percent of the class who had goals but not plans were earning, on an average, twice as much as the 84 percent who had no goals at all. The 3 percent who had clear goals and a plan to achieve them were earning ten times more than the remaining 97 percent put together!

Mold your future with well-defined goals and a roadmap to achieve them.

Setting well-defined goals with a clear roadmap to achieve them has the power to mold your future the way you want it to be. Unless you plan your success and change your track from the normal flow of life, your life will be ordinary. If you want to live an extraordinary life, you will have to create your own flow and determine your destination in advance.

DIFFERENT TYPES OF GOALS AND QUESTIONS

We now know the importance of deadlines, the hierarchy of goals, and the potential of written goals and plans. Let's explore the different types of goals with a short exercise for each type.

Write down your answers to questions given in the exercise. Be honest, as these questions will guide you toward understanding and achieving your goals. Spend some time thinking about the questions. Let your subconscious mind give you the answer. Remember, there's no right or wrong answer.

There are ten types of goals.

1. Goals for Self

Personal goals will lead to character development. They help you understand who you are and drive you to analyze what you want to leave behind as your legacy. You must identify your strengths and weaknesses to achieve your personal goals.

Personal goals improve your relationship with yourself. You will see self-improvement with the satisfaction of your personal goals. There will be a noticeable change in your attitude. Your outlook toward life will be a lot more positive.

Achieving personal goals will aid you in living practically and increasing your emotional quotient.

Exercise:

1. What is your biggest dream, vision, or hope for yourself and how can you convert it into reality?

2. If you could wake up tomorrow having one specific ability, what it would be?

3. How would you like to start your day?

4. What would you eliminate to make your life simpler?

5. What would you like for your birthday gift this year?

2. *Goals for Your Health*

Your body is the only thing that is truly yours; everything else is materialistic. Your health goals determine how you work toward preserving your body. They pertain to goals related to diet, fitness, addictions, and physical appearance. *Health is wealth* is a cliché, but it cannot be truer.

Health goals deal with things that will directly or indirectly affect your health. Your diet, addictions, sleeping patterns, and their internal manifestations like heart rate, cholesterol, body mass index, etc. form a part of health goals.

Exercise:

1. What would you like your body to look and feel like at the age of seventy?

2. How often would you like to get a medical checkup?

3. Which unhealthy habit would you like to give up today?

4. What type of exercise program would you like to start?

5. What seems physically impossible for you today but would change your life completely if you could do it?

3. *Goals for Family*

Your family goals bring the right balance in your life. Family goals can help strengthen your bond with your spouse, parents, children, and relatives. They help you analyze your contribution to the family. These goals determine whether you are an asset or a liability for your family.

The exercise below helps you set goals related to initiating, strengthening, clarifying, and enhancing your relationship with your family members.

Exercise:

1. In what ways can you be less selfish in your relationship with your spouse?

2. What hobbies, activities, or intellectual pursuits would you like your spouse to engage in with you?

3. What can you do to make dinnertime a fun family experience?

4. What games and activities can you engage in with your children?

5. What would you like to do for your parents to make their lives more enjoyable?

4. Goals for Friendship

Friends are an integral part of our lives. Defining friendship goals helps you maintain your relationship with old friends and form new ones. Understanding and achieving your friendship goals helps you build a strong relationship with likeminded people.

Meeting your friendship goals is as important as meeting family goals.

Friendship is all about enjoying each other's company. It is about maintaining networks and helping each other. Friends are like the family that you get to choose, so meeting your friendship goals is as important as meeting family goals.

Exercise:

1. With whom would you like to get in contact, even if you haven't spoken in years?

2. What can you do to be in better contact with old friends?

3. Which relationships should you end altogether?

4. What things would you like to share with your friends?

5. What would you like to do to make your best friend's next birthday a special experience?

5. *Goals for the Community*

We take a lot from our community, and it is our duty to give back something to our community. We have an obligation to people other than our family, relatives, and friends.

Community goals help you understand your social responsibility in a better manner and help you serve society. In order to fulfil your community goals you will have to take time out from your busy schedule. The right way to engage in accomplishing community goals is to take the help of family and friends to achieve them. In that way, you can spend some quality time with them while serving the community.

Exercise:

1. With what charitable organization would you like to get involved?

2. What small acts of kindness and courtesy can you do to make life easier/more enjoyable for others?

3. What political, social, or moral cause would you like to be involved in?

4. How can you influence people to opt for community service?

5. What possessions that you no longer have use for could be given to the needy?

6. *Goals for Your Career*

You spend one third of your life at work, so it is extremely important to choose a vocation that suits your abilities and your likes. Making a career in your desirable field requires a lot of planning. Career goals help you identify strategic objectives and appropriate activities for skill and career development.

Setting smart career goals makes life secure for you and your family. Career goals are important to build collegial relationships and reach the level you had envisioned for yourself when you first started working.

Exercise:

1. What specific things can you do, change, or eliminate to become better at work?

2. What occupational certifications would you like to achieve?

3. What series of jobs, levels, and positions do you want to attain at your place of work?

4. What type of work would you be like to be doing five years from now?

5. What could you do that would help you communicate your ideas more effectively at work?

7. *Goals for Financial Stability*

Financial goals pertain to material wealth and satisfaction. We live in a world that functions on money. Determining your financial goals, therefore, gives you the right direction and helps you figure out ways to reach there in time. Financial goals cater to the entire circle of earnings, savings, investments, and expenditure.

Establishing well-defined financial goals helps you ascertain how much your annual earnings should be. It allows you to set aside money for short- and long-term needs. Managing your finances helps you lead a relaxed, retired life.

Exercise:

1. How much money would you like to earn this year? In five years? In ten years?

2. What can you do to generate more income in addition to your work salary?

3. How much money would you like to save in an emergency fund?

4. At what age would you like to retire?

5. What will be the sources of your income when you are retired?

8. *Goals for Your Home*

These goals revolve around your biggest investment—your house. It is often said that there is no place like home. Most of the best moments in a person's life are spent in his/her home. Household goals help you keep your home the center of excitement in your life. You can manage your household needs and expenses easily once you analyze your household goals.

Exercise:

1. What would your ideal home look and feel like?

2. What precautionary measures will you take to safeguard your house?

3. How can you make your home more energy efficient?

4. What creative things can you do to make your housework fun and quick?

5. How would you like the interiors of your house to be?

9. Goals for the Soul

Spiritual goals lead to your peace of mind. Spirituality affects your decisions. Setting spiritual goals helps you lead a peaceful life. When one gets spiritually awakened, the ramifications are felt in daily life as well. One becomes calm and composed in every aspect of one's life and reaps a lot of benefits.

Exercise:

1. What spiritual qualities would you like to develop?

2. What would you like to learn about religion and spirituality?

3. What would you like to teach your family members about spirituality?

4. What spiritual material would you like to read about?

5. How much time would you like to spend meditating or praying on a daily basis?

10. Goals for Recreation

Recreation goals add vitality and a whole new dimension to your lifestyle. They help you relax and rejuvenate in order to renew your energy to achieve the rest of the goals. These goals allow you to express yourselves creatively. Understand your recreation goals and get in touch with your inner self.

You can widen your horizons by achieving your recreational goals. Recreation goals comprise things like learning to play a musical instrument, going on a hike, travelling to exotic locations, etc. Such activities provide your body with much-needed rest and rejuvenate your mind for the challenges ahead.

Exercise:

1. Where would you like to go on your next vacation?

2. What parts or activities of your city or community would you like to visit or take part in?

3. Which major sporting events or concerts would you like to attend this year?

4. Which television programs are positive for you to watch and which ones should you avoid?

5. What recreational games would you like to play?

Achieving four or five
of the ten goals and
neglecting the others
won't serve the purpose.

A JUGGLER'S ACT

Life is all about maintaining the right balance. The ten goals mentioned above constitute the major goals in life. Achieving four or five of them and neglecting the others won't serve the purpose. You need to achieve all the goals to maintain the balance, as they are closely interlinked. They are interdependent. One achieves the ultimate goal of life when one fulfils all the ten goals.

The exercise given under each goal will open your mind and force you to think about your goals from a different perspective. It is imperative to answer those questions with utmost honesty to derive the benefits.

Once you have answered all the 50 questions, you will see your goals in front of you along with a roadmap that will take you toward your goals. These goals define your purpose at every stage of your life. From there onward, it's a juggler's act of balancing all ten goals.

CHAPTER REWIND

- Personal goals improve your relationship with yourself.

- Your health goals determine how you work toward preserving your body.

- Your family goals bring the right balance in your life.

- Understanding and achieving your friendship goals helps you build strong relationships with likeminded people.

- Community goals help you understand your social responsibility in a better manner and help you serve the society.

- Career goals help you identify strategic objectives and appropriate activities for skill and career development.

- Financial goals cater to the entire circle of earnings, savings, investments, and expenditure.

- Household goals help you keep your home the center of excitement in your life.

- Spiritual goals lead to your peace of mind.

- Recreation goals add vitality and a whole new dimension to your lifestyle.

Chapter 3

PATHWAY TO GLORY

*"Vision without action is a daydream.
Action without vision is a nightmare."*
—JAPANESE PROVERB

SEE IT TO BE IT

In the year 1976, a news reporter met Arnold Schwarzenegger and asked him about his future goals. At that time, Arnold was only known in the bodybuilding circuit and had not started acting in movies. He had retired as a bodybuilder after reaching great heights, so the reporter wanted to know about his plans for the future.

Schwarzenegger replied that his next goal was to be the number-one movie star in Hollywood. The reporter was shocked by his answer. Arnold was an all-muscle guy, with no acting background, poor communication skills, and a heavy Austrian accent. The reporter found it hard to imagine Arnold in Hollywood. He asked Arnold how he planned to convert his dream into reality.

Arnold said that he would approach his goal of being a premier movie star in the same manner he approached his goal of becoming the number-one bodybuilder in the world. His approach was pretty simple—create a vision of what he wanted to be and start living like that, as if it were true. He created a vision for himself and lived every moment like that until the vision became reality.

Arnold Schwarzenegger did become one of Hollywood's superstars. He saw it to be it. You only get one life to live, so why not live the best life possible? Remember, if you can see it, you can be it.

You only get one life to live, so why not live the best life possible?

We are what we think we are. Psychologists state that our self-image impacts our every decision. If you don't think you will be successful, you won't. You have to see it to be it. Changing your life starts with changing the vision of your life.

BEING SMARTER IN GOAL SETTING

You know goals are crucial for converting your dreams into reality. But how do you set well-defined goals? The

SMARTER model explains the characteristics of goals so you understand your goals better and set smarter ones.

1. S—Specific

Your goals cannot be vague; they need to be specific. You must be clear as to what you want from a particular goal. What do you want to achieve? Your vision also has to be specific, full of details. For example, if your goal is to buy a new house, specify the details to yourself. Think about the number of rooms in the house, the colors, the interiors, the garden, the pool, and so on.

Specifying your goals curtails wishful thinking and allows you to concentrate on the goal. Once you have the specific aspects of your goal, write it down and place it such that it is always visible to you. In this way, your subconscious mind will always be reminded of your specific goal.

2. M—Measurable

Your progress toward your goals must be measurable. If we cannot measure it, we cannot accomplish it. Measuring your progress can act as a source of motivation as well. If you think your progress is not up to the mark, you can change your strategy accordingly.

In certain type of goals, it may not be possible to measure your progress. Spiritual and relationship goals are intangible; thus it is difficult to measure our effort under such goals. In such cases, you can note down and keep a track of the activities that you are doing to advance toward those goals.

3. A—Attainable

You need to set challenging goals that can be attainable. Goals should be out of reach to be challenging but not out of sight. If your goals are out of sight, they will only result in disappointment. Goals need to be such that they motivate you to meet your potential.

Sometimes people set goals to impress others. They set farfetched goals in order to blame the magnitude of the goal for their failure. Set goals that are difficult but not impossible. Goals should be attainable; otherwise, they will lead to frustration and negativity.

4. R—Realistic

Realistic goals are important to distinguish between fantasies and goals. Getting six-pack abs can be realistic. But if you want six-pack abs overnight, it is a fantasy; it is unrealistic. Unrealistic goals are a waste of time. You need to focus and channel your energy on attaining realistic goals.

5. T—Time Bound

Your goals must have a timeline. They should have a starting time and an ending time. You are investing your time when you are pursuing your goals. Ensuring that your goals have a deadline helps you stay away from procrastinating and yields good returns on your investment.

Your goals can be short-term (one year), medium-term (up to three years), or long-term (up to five years). You can break them down into monthly, weekly, or daily goals too. When you achieve daily goals on a consistent level, it will ultimately result in achieving weekly, monthly, and yearly goals.

6. E—Execution

This is the most important part of the model. You have planned meticulously, considered all the options, and chosen a route toward your goal. Without execution, you won't be able to reach there. To see your goals right to the end requires an immense amount of faith in your goals and conviction in your abilities.

7. R—Rewarding

When you understand the rewards associated with the accomplishment of your goals, they will keep you motivated to achieve them. Ask yourself what you are going to derive after attaining a particular goal. The answer can be tangible or intangible. Whatever it might be, your answer is your reward for the immense hard work and determination that you put in. Keep thinking about the reward and it will not let you down.

This SMARTER model of goal setting will clear your mind and provide you with a different perspective and outline to achieve your goals.

THE FOUR-WAY TEST

The four-way test consists of 24 words that will guide you to achieve your goals. They will assure you that you are on a righteous path and that your goal is going to add value to your social circle rather than being detrimental to it. It is a template for successful problem solving. Ask yourself the following four questions, and let these 24 words lead you on a journey to meet your goals:

- Is it the truth?

- Is it fair to all concerned?

- Will it build goodwill and better friendships?

- Will it be beneficial to all concerned?

Let's look at developing precise goals for ourselves. Your answers to the questions in the second chapter might have given you a fair idea of what the important goals in your life are. Follow this goal development program to achieve the right balance between all types of goals.

You are in the best position to judge yourself.

Unmask

Many people roam around wearing a mask. Some face society wearing a mask. Some even have different masks for their work, family, or friends. The mask may reflect positivity and success, but the true face may be scared and fragile. Those who wear a mask know the difference between what is true and what is not.

It is important to unmask while setting a goal because only you know who you are and where you are. You are in the best position to judge yourself. Remember that this is your starting point; it is going to be the foundation of your goal. If you are going to corrupt it with a false image, your goals will never materialize.

Understand your strengths and weaknesses. Refer to Abraham Maslow's need pyramid and identify the stage you are at and the type of goals you are concentrating on. Make use of the answers that you had written for each type of goal to understand your beginning and ending points.

The Wish List

After you remove your mask, you will be able to travel from the start to the end with a truthful and honest approach. Take a pen and paper and write down all your desires and wishes pertaining to a particular type of goal. Do it for every type of goal. Begin with your most urgent category and jot down things required to achieve that goal.

This wish list need not be structured. Just note down whatever comes to your mind regarding a particular type of goal. It can include tangible as well as intangible items. Try to visualize your wants and rewards to perfection. Provide necessary details if required.

Why Why Why?

After a lot of wishful thinking, it is time to put some rationale in this process. Ask yourself why you want a particular thing you have listed. Is it because of your needs or society's needs? Many lives are wasted chasing unwanted dreams. People struggle for their entire lifetime running behind a goal that wasn't theirs to begin with. It is important to know whether the goals you are setting are yours or someone else's.

If you are unable to find a logical answer for a point mentioned in your list, discard it. You may ask, "Why go through the process of listing a particular item only to discard it in the end?" This process helps you realize that even though you wanted a particular goal, you had the smartness and the responsibility to reject it in order to meet a substantial goal.

Balance the Scale

For the remaining items on the list, see whether attaining these goals will further your ultimate objective of maintaining the balance in your life. All types of goals need to be balanced. Think whether concentrating or rejecting a particular goal will stabilize other goals or cause an upheaval. Make sure that you have adequate time, energy, and money to meet other types of goals as well.

Manage

Manage your time, energy, and money effectively and efficiently. Choose how much time, energy, and money you are going to invest in each goal. It will give you a clear picture regarding your present and the future. Use your past to judge your present and future expenditure and manage your time, energy, and money to attain short-term, medium-term, and long-term goals.

Follow this goal development method for every type of goal and you will be ready to live the life you always wanted to live. This exercise tells you that you have the power to decide what you want from life. Until now, life was dictating terms to you, but after constructing your goals and embarking on the path to accomplish them, you can dictate terms to life. The power is in your hands.

SOCRATES AND THE SUCCESS SECRET

A boy was travelling with the great Greek philosopher Socrates. He took the opportunity to ask the philosopher the secret of success. Socrates smiled at him and told the boy to meet him by the river next morning. The boy was thrilled to know that Socrates was going to tell him the secret. The boy couldn't sleep for the entire night and reached the riverside early.

Socrates met him and asked to walk with him toward the river. The boy obliged and they started walking. They reached the end of the bank, but Socrates didn't stop walking. Cold water touched their feet, but they kept walking. It rose to their knees, but they still kept wading. It was getting difficult to march through the river. The water level rose to their waists but they were still moving forward. The boy struggled to keep pace, but Socrates stared into the vast river and continued walking peacefully.

The boy didn't want to miss out on the secret to success, so he matched pace with Socrates and walked into the river until the water level rose to their necks. The boy looked at Socrates questioningly and Socrates answered him by ducking him into the water. The boy struggled and tried to get away from the philosopher's grip, but his efforts were in vain.

It was just a matter of time before the water would enter his lungs and the boy would drown. After struggling for a while, the boy gave up and stopped moving, resigned to his fate. At that precise moment, Socrates loosened his grip and allowed the boy to rise above the water. The boy took a deep breath of air. Socrates then ensured that the boy was out of the river and fully recovered.

When you want success as badly as you need the air, you will get it.

After he was out of the river, Socrates asked the boy what he wanted the most when he was drowning and suffocating. The boy said that he just wanted to breathe in some air. Socrates smiled and told him that that was the secret of success. When you want success as badly as you need the air, you will get it.

JOURNEY TO GLORY

Now you have defined your goals. How do you go about achieving them? Just as you make the journey to reach your destination to reach your goals, you need to follow your plan. Your action plan is the pathway to glory. To follow your plan, you will need to:

Recharge Your Battery

Wanting something is not enough; you must be possessed by it. Your motivation must be absolutely compelling in order to overcome the obstacles that will invariably come your way. Your goals should be the purpose of your life. They should keep you motivated and charged up.

There will come a time when everything will turn dark and gloomy. At that time, think about the rewards that you are going to get once you accomplish your goal. Use them as a motivational tool. Fear is generally associated with negativity, but you can channel fear into something positive. You can use it as a motivational tool. Start with determination to end up with satisfaction.

100 Percent Commitment

Commit and surrender to your goals. Desire is the key to motivation, but it is unrelenting determination and commitment that will enable you to attain the success you seek. You can write down your goals and place them where you can see them frequently to remind you of your commitment to the cause.

Another way to commit to your goals is to share them with your near and dear ones. They will support you in your pursuit and remind you about your goals.

Hop, Skip, Jump

Difficulties help you strengthen your mind. Challenges are bound to be there, but what matters is your attitude toward those challenges. Identify the challenges that can come toward you and prepare to overcome them in advance. The only thing you can do after identifying challenges is to prepare yourself and anticipate them. The challenges will occur at their own time and pace. You have to focus on your goal and adapt to the situation to overcome them.

The Student Attitude

You will need specific skills for specific tasks. Be resourceful in your approach. Overcoming certain challenges may involve learning new skills. Do not hesitate to learn something new if it is going to help you achieve your goal. Remain a student throughout your life. Certain tasks may demand revisiting old tricks. Stay positive and open to new and old resources to get the job done.

Do not hesitate to learn something new if it is going to help you achieve your goal.

People Person

Enhance your people skills. Along the pathway, you will require the help of a variety of people. Although your goals are personal, achieving them requires a team effort. A lot of people are directly or indirectly involved in the process.

Family, friends, neighbors, colleagues, etc. will interact with you and touch you in some way or the other during the pursuit of your goals. Only when you are able to collaborate with them positively will you be able to progress toward your goal.

True to Self

Set timelines and be accountable to your goals. Break the goals into short-term, medium-term, and long-term plans. Take baby steps toward you goals and be accountable for them. Remember that it is your goal and you are going to reap benefits after achieving it. Stick to the plan and face the consequences if your goals are not met in the specified timeline. In case things do not go as planned, work on a different action plan instead of engaging in the blame game.

Disciplined to a T

Discipline is the bridge between forming goals and accomplishing them. Every day there will be a new challenge. The dynamics of the game will change unceremoniously. Staying disciplined will help you through thick and thin. It will remind you of the larger purpose and help you focus on your target. A disciplined outlook will strengthen you and protect you from being lazy.

Active Lifestyle

An active lifestyle will keep your body well oiled. Your body as well as your mind needs to be healthy. An active lifestyle is a culmination of physical and mental health. It will ensure that you stay positive, have a good self-image, and stay disciplined and motivated. Reading positive books and/or religious scriptures will contribute immensely in a subconscious manner.

Elastic

Be flexible in your approach. Not every plan is going to work. There will be hiccups along the way. The best bet is to make sure that there is a backup plan. It is important to stick to your decisions and modify your directions. Failure tells you that things need to be done differently. If you face a roadblock, simply take another route to your destination.

The Reward Therapy

Reward yourself when you achieve small goals. This will help you celebrate your success, enhance your self-confidence, and stay motivated. Take a break, refresh, and get back to work. This small string of achieving goals and celebrating them will eventually lead to reaching your ultimate goal and the ultimate reward.

Follow this pathway to accomplish every goal. Once you have achieved a goal, revisit this pathway and do the same things over and over again until you have reached your ultimate goal.

CHAPTER REWIND
CHAPTER REWIND

- If you can see it, you can be it.

- Check if your goal is yours.

- Choose how much time, energy, and money you are going to invest in each goal.

- After constructing your goals and embarking on the path to accomplish them, you can dictate terms to life.

- Start with determination to end up with satisfaction.

- Unrelenting determination and commitment will enable you to attain the success you seek.

- Challenges are bound to be there, but what matters is your attitude toward those challenges.

- Do not hesitate to learn something new if it is going to help you achieve your goal.

- Break the goals into short-term, medium-term, and long-term plans.

- Discipline is the bridge between forming goals and accomplishing them.

- If you face a roadblock, simply take another route to your destination.

- Plan, work, achieve, and celebrate.

Chapter 4

Overcoming Roadblocks

"If you can find a path with no obstacles,
it probably doesn't lead anywhere."
—Frank A. Clark

ARTHUR'S MISTAKE

Arthur was always late to school. He was the last to enter a class or to submit an assignment or a project. He was the last for everything. One day, one of his teachers set the class a challenging project, but gave them adequate time to complete it. As usual, Arthur missed the deadline. This time he was petrified. He thought the teacher would complain to the principal about his slothfulness. He came to class and found out that he was the only one who had not submitted the project. He thought he was in for detention this time.

The teacher asked Arthur calmly why he had not submitted the project. He said that he had to attend a family function, so he couldn't complete the project. The teacher surprisingly remained calm and advised him that one must anticipate events, plan accordingly, and avoid delaying their work.

He requested an extension and the teacher gave it to him on the condition that he would submit all the remaining assignments with this project. Arthur agreed and asked the teacher for a deadline. He was in for a shock when the teacher said the deadline was the next day.

That day, there was a huge celebration in school, which he had to miss because he had to complete his projects. The entire school was celebrating, but Arthur was burning the midnight oil to complete his projects. He would have been at the party if he had not procrastinated and completed his work on time.

If procrastination is not avoided, then you will always be playing catch up and pay a hefty price in the end.

This might seem a minor incident because it happened at a school level. What if it happens at an organizational level? It might even cost you your job. If procrastination is not avoided, you will always be playing catch up and pay a hefty price in the end.

THE SHADOW OF PROCRASTINATION

Procrastination is the act of delaying things indefinitely. You might say to yourself that you will complete a particular task tomorrow, but that "tomorrow" never comes. Procrastination stops you from earning more money, befriending people, maintaining relationships, and staying happy.

Procrastination keeps you in the dark and stops you from venturing into the light. It is a shadow that follows you even in the dark. It stops you from reaching your goals and rewards. Initially, you might feel good to delay things and enjoy the free time, but procrastination strikes back like a venomous snake in the end.

We might find ourselves delaying taking action on our goals because we are not in the right mood, we are unable to prioritize, or we are simply lazy. But we have to eradicate the root cause of procrastination and avoid falling in the trap.

LET THERE BE LIGHT

The first step toward solving a problem is to acknowledge the fact that you have a problem. Acknowledge that you procrastinate and then make an action plan to overcome it. You are procrastinating if you feel that things are not panning out as they were supposed to. You are procrastinating if you are not achieving things on time, if you rush to finish things at the last moment, if you make plans but fail to take any action to accomplish those plans, and if you have a goal in mind but the body doesn't move toward it.

Identify the precise reason that is stopping you from working toward those goals. It can be one reason or a combination of reasons that might be stopping you. Once you find the reason, think about the opportunity cost. Think about what you would've done with the time you wasted. You could have spent that time to reach a step closer to your goal. You could have spent that time with your children, investing money, traveling, swimming, playing guitar, working out, planning retirement, or working hard to reach your ultimate goal.

ERADICATE THE SHADOW

The most common reason for procrastinating is the lazy mood. We say we are not in the mood to do things. It is not even a reason; it is an excuse. We look for an excuse to avoid doing our work. We say that we are too tired to do a particular task; we will do it once we get refreshed or after we finish dinner. Then, after the time comes, we say, "Now it is too late; let's do it tomorrow," and then the same cycle follows again. Do you find yourself looking for some excuse to avoid doing things?

High energy levels will make sure that you overcome the initial resistance and then carry on with the task once you have started.

How do we do it? We move on. We can get in the right mood by scheduling such activities at a time when our energy levels are high. It can be any time of the day.

High energy levels will make sure that you overcome the initial resistance and then carry on with the task you have started. Many people face difficulty going to the gym in the early morning. The trick to avoid it is to get out of bed as soon as you are awake. Once you find yourself out of bed and wide awake, you will have no problem whatsoever going to the gym.

Many people delay things because of fear. When the task is out of their comfort zone, it becomes a major concern. Whatever the fear may be, the only way to get rid of fear is to take action. Fear keeps growing when you go on thinking about the tasks you have to do. You need to act as quickly as possible. Your subconscious has already gone through the process of thinking. It is due to procrastination that you are not able to translate those thoughts into actions. You have to visualize yourself being brave and then act accordingly.

In order to overcome procrastination, it is important to realize that you are not gunning for perfectionism. Nobody is perfect; the results do not matter as much the effort. You just need to concentrate on the effort part and leave the results to the universe. The pressure of being perfect stops us from executing our ideas. Avoid procrastination by admitting that you are not perfect and perfectionism is not what you are looking for. Tell yourself that you are looking for a satisfactory result in proportion to the effort that you are putting in.

Another way of procrastinating is by doing mundane activities instead of focusing on the productive ones. People try to cheat themselves by whiling away time, performing a low priority task instead of doing a high priority task. You might find yourself lost in the Internet when you are supposed to concentrate on an important assignment. Routine tasks are important, but you need to manage them well. Engaging in routine tasks is just another way of making excuses to avoid working on the larger task at hand. Keeping a tab on your activities and arranging them priority-wise will enable you to focus on your goal and avoid procrastination.

THE BRAIN CONUNDRUM

Our brain plays tricks on us all the time. Scientists have not been able to decipher the true power of the human brain. Our brain is brilliant but sometimes it can catch us off guard. Very often, our instinctive reactions are counterproductive. Sometimes, our brain's natural reaction to certain situations does more to sabotage than help. We must learn to combat our brain's natural reaction and take action according to the situation.

Dark Fantasy

Our brain ruins our goals by fantasizing about them. You may say that fantasizing or visualizing is a good trait. Not in the case when our brain overdoes it. It converts our fantasies into dark fantasies. The negative aspect of fantasizing is that it prompts us to perceive success as if it has already been achieved. We anticipate it in the present when in reality we have not even started working toward it. These fantasies leave us with no motivation, as we feel we have already achieved our goals. Do not give up on your dream, but do not fall under its spell as well.

Zeigarnik Effect

Psychological research conducted by Russian psychologist Bluma Zeigarnik suggests that we are better at remembering things that are partially done. We can use the Zeigarnik Effect to fight against our brain's procrastination. Under this study, people were given puzzles to solve and were stopped midway. They were asked to remember where they had stopped. People remembered where they had stopped with utmost confidence.

Another study asked people to solve a puzzle, and they were given unlimited time to do so. When people were trying to solve it, they were interrupted by stating that their time was over. Despite the time stoppage, many people continued to solve the puzzle as their brain wanted it to be solved.

Once we start with a task, our brain is wired to finish it.

This theory is also used by television shows to keep the audience hanging at the end. They long for more and end up watching the subsequent episode. This is because our brain longs for conclusion. So, once we start with a task, our brain is wired in a way to finish it. Thus, we can beat procrastination by starting our intended task, and as our brain already thinks that the task is interesting it will strive hard to complete it.

Mission Abort

Imagine you are on a strict diet. You have done pretty well to stay away from alluring food. Now, your defense is about to be tested, as you are scheduled to go to a friend's party. Instead of a home cooked meal, you are compelled to eat outside food. It is a party, so you cannot avoid binging. Your host forces you to have some unhealthy snacks and your diet goes off track.

To balance that out, you know that you should eat something healthy, probably a salad, but having tasted fried stuff, your brain prompts you to go for the burger instead of the salad. On the slightest derailment, your brain forces you to abort the mission. It tells you to forget about your goal and commit to something that you have been running away from all this time. Don't give your brain a chance to abort the mission—resist temptations and you are sure to achieve your goals.

Reinforcement

Backup plans act as reinforcements. Psychologists have found out that our brain functions better when we have contingency plans in place. Backup plans provide a cushioning to our brain and it continues to move toward the goal, even if the first plan doesn't materialize. We should ensure that our goals have backup plans in case of emergencies.

The punishment method also works well on your brain. Suppose you falter on your way toward your goal; instead of abandoning ship, you should put in an extra effort and punish your brain for faltering.

Our brain can trick us, but we have to be its master and always be in control.

Overcoming Barriers

When everything is coming your way, you are probably driving in the wrong lane. Even when you are driving in the right lane, there will be roadblocks, rash drivers, detours, deviations, unforeseen circumstances, weather changes, etc. You do not stop driving because of the barriers, right? In the same fashion, there will be barriers in front of you when you are in pursuit of your goals. You have to continue your journey and make necessary adjustments to reach your destination.

Keep Faith

Faith is taking the first step even when the path in front of you is unclear. Faith is what will guide you through your entire journey. There will be dark phases in your journey, but faith is what will keep the little candle burning. Trust your instincts and believe in your purpose. It is said that the night is the darkest just before the dawn.

Having faith will allow you to concentrate on what you have instead of concentrating on what you should or would have. Faith will allow you to take control of your life and lend a strong support to you when things go out of control.

Take Diversion

Use diversions when you face roadblocks, but do not stop. Take rest, rejuvenate, and start over. If one strategy does not work, think of another one. Remember that there is no perfect way. There are multiple ways to lead you to your destination and the only condition is that you must give your hundred percent and never give up.

Procrastinate Positively

Until now, we were considering procrastination as a negative trait, but you can also use it positively. Many times, you will come across situations that will demand urgent actions. In such situations, you might have to concentrate on a different type of goal. If there is a financial crisis, then you will have to concentrate on meeting your financial goal instead of focusing your energy on, say, recreational goals. At that time, you will have to positively and willfully procrastinate and give your full attention to specific goals.

Try Answering

Rather than focusing on the questions, focus on the answers. Think about solutions all the time when you hit a roadblock, rather than thinking about the barriers. Thinking about answers will change your perception, and eventually you will find an answer to overcome the barrier.

In such situations, you may think either positively or negatively. Negativity forces you to stay where you are, whereas positivity adds mobility to your goals. When you are in a positive frame of mind, you can come up with innovative ways to overcome the barrier. Problems will always be there; what matters is your attitude toward them.

Negativity forces you to stay where you are, whereas positivity adds mobility to your goals.

Set a Speed Limit

You might have noticed that highways have speed limits. On your journey toward your goals, your attitude toward your barriers will determine your speed limit. Your approach will determine at what pace you travel and reach your destination.

You are given a free pass to drive as fast as you can. The choice is up to you whether you want to stop and ponder over every roadblock with a negative attitude or whiz past it with a positive attitude. Twenty percent of the speed limit may be defined externally, but you define the remaining eighty percent.

Uninstall

We learn about things while growing up. We learn things that have a positive impact on us as well as things that have a negative impact on us. Just as a computer installs or uninstalls software, we have the ability to learn and unlearn things.

Practicing things on a daily basis will help us gain mastery over a particular task. Similarly, abandoning things will force us to forget how we used to function with them. Uninstall your negative traits and unlearn all the negative things that do not allow you to rise from the quicksand of negativity.

Challenge Comfort Zone

Get out of your comfort zone to explore new opportunities. Comfort zones are barriers by themselves. They stop you from progressing. Whenever you are in your comfort zone, you end up resisting change. You do not consider whether the change is positive or negative; you cut it out altogether. Life reaches a stagnant point when we settle in our comfort zone. It is evolutionary for mankind to change and change for the better.

A comfort zone is nothing but a trap set by our mind to stop us from progressing. However, the trap also has a latch to let yourself out. You just have to reach out and escape from the trap for your success.

Drill

Keep on drilling until you reach the core of the barrier. Addressing the issue superficially is a temporary solution, but drilling and reaching its core to uproot it is a permanent one. Uprooting the barrier from its roots will ensure that it does not crop up again. You may spend considerable time and energy in finding and reaching the root cause of the problem. It is all right, because at the end you won't have to deal with it again.

It is of utmost importance to apply the right solution to the right problem. Fixing a problem with the wrong tools only leads to delay. It doesn't serve the purpose. You must find the right tools and approach to handle a particular situation.

Revise

Revise and review the obstacle as a goal. Focus all your energy to get through. Once you start looking at an obstacle as a goal, you will undergo the process of planning and executing goals meticulously and emerge as a winner. You can approach the problem itself as a short-term goal and apply the relevant tactics and strategies to overcome it. Change your perception toward your barriers to get the desired results.

Use the tricks and techniques mentioned above to overcome roadblocks and continue the pursuit of your goals. Remember to strive hard persistently and never give up.

CHAPTER REWIND

CHAPTER REWIND

- Procrastination keeps you in the dark and stops you from venturing into the light.

- Do not give up on your dreams, but do not fall under their spell either.

- Don't give your brain a chance to abort the mission; resist temptations and you are sure to achieve your goals.

- There will be dark phases in your journey, but faith is what will keep the little candle burning.

- Think about solutions all the time when you hit a roadblock, rather than thinking about the barriers.

- Fixing a problem with the wrong tools only leads to delay.

- Change your perception toward your barriers to get the desired results.

Chapter 5

MANAGE TIME, MANAGE LIFE

*"It's better to do the right thing slowly
than the wrong thing quickly."*
—PETER TURLA

THE INTERVIEW FOR AN HEIR

Mr. Banks was about to retire, leaving his vast empire heirless. The multi-billionaire businessman had lost his family in a fatal plane crash. He did not wish to offer the post of the Chief Operating Officer (CEO) of his business to a relative just because they shared the same bloodline. His able secretary had carried out a stringent interview process that selected the best candidates from around the world.

The selection criteria comprised and surpassed the regular conditions like quantitative ability, psychometric tests, intellectual and emotional quotient, etc. The candidates were narrowed down to three and their final test was about to be revealed. The trio awaited Mr. Banks in a brightly-lit conference room. The room was comprised of the quintessential round table and three seats. There was absolute silence, so much so that the trio could hear their heartbeats, which escalated as the door opened to reveal Mr. Banks in a white suit.

He walked swiftly to the whiteboard and wrote in an unruly handwriting, "Which is the most perishable item in this corporate world? You have three hours to find the answer; once you are done, meet me in my cabin on the third floor." He wrote this and walked past the candidates like they were invisible and closed the door.

The three candidates—a young graduate with business experience, a vice president of a small company, and a young CEO—stared at the board after glancing at each other. The generous three-hour deadline baffled them more than the question. The neurons in their brain went into a hyperactive state and they began to feel restless, nervous, and anxious. The vice president tried to ascertain various clauses of the test, whereas the CEO looked at it from a universal angle. Meanwhile, the young girl stood up from the seat, passed the two men toward the door, opened it gently, and went through in just five minutes. The remaining two candidates laughed at the girl for being naïve and continued to rattle their brains for the entire duration without finding an answer.

After the deadline, Mr. Banks entered the conference room and declared that the two candidates had failed to answer the question in three hours, whereas the girl had answered it in just five minutes. She had been chosen as the CEO. This left the two candidates fuming and they demanded an explanation.

Mr. Banks explained that the answer to his question is *time* and the girl valued it by answering the question within five minutes without overanalyzing the situation and ending up without an answer like the two men. As the vice president and CEO were walking out, Mr. Banks said, "Respect time; otherwise it will not respect you."

Time is of great importance because it can only be utilized at that precise moment.

Time is of great importance because it can only be utilized at that precise moment. The value of an unused minute drops to zero when the moment passes. Make every minute count by managing your time effectively and efficiently.

VALUE OF EMPTY SEAT

Airports are always buzzing with excitement. You can see people arriving, departing, and waiting, and the airport staff busily moving about their routine. Everything happens according to time. A slight delay in a particular activity derails the entire schedule for the day.

Every airplane has a limited number of seats, and they try to fly as much as possible to gain profit. The seats have different prices, and they fill up accordingly. Once the plane takes off with an empty seat, the value of that seat is zero. It doesn't matter if the empty seat is in economy or business class; the opportunity to cash in on it is gone. A seat is only valued when it is paid for. An empty seat has no value. Once the plane takes off, there is no way one can generate profit from the empty seats. The opportunity is lost. The same principal can be applied to our life.

Each one of us has a specific amount of time assigned for every task. If we do not act in the time designated for that moment, it is lost forever. It is not going to come back. It is like the empty seat. Lost or wasted time can never be recovered.

RACE AGAINST THE CLOCK

As long as you are on earth, you have twenty-four hours in a day. Many people find it difficult to accomplish their everyday tasks in those twenty-four hours. But how do the others do it? After all, they also have just twenty-four hours at their disposal. The answer lies in effective time management. Successful people manage their time successfully.

People feel overloaded and often work late to meet their deadlines. Their day begins with a crisis and ends with one. They always seem to be low on energy and depressed. Let's see why people complain about lack of time.

To-Do List

Many times people fail to meet their deadlines because they do not prepare a list of tasks they have to perform. They have large projects in hand but they fail to list the small goals that will take them toward their larger goal.

It is not just about making goals, it is about writing them down so that you know about them. When people do not have a list, they concentrate on any random task and in the end fail to complete the project or live up to expectations.

Reining in the Goals

People tend to fumble when they do not manage their goals. They need to segregate their goals into short-term, medium-term, and long-term goals and allocate a duration for each of them. Without a defined time, there would be no difference between a short-term goal and a long-term goal.

When you don't have an assigned duration, you may end up spending a lot of time on your short-term goals and eventually fail to meet your long-term goals.

This One or That One?

This is a major time management pitfall. People keep performing tasks that are not due in the near future. They fail to prioritize and in turn do not meet deadlines for the scheduled tasks.

Suppose you are asked to prepare a presentation for the sales pitch that is due for the next day and to figure out an advertising strategy, which you need by next week. Let's say you are busy with the creative team figuring out the advertising strategy instead of working on the presentation. You will fail to complete the presentation in time and your boss will definitely not be pleased with you.

In this case, both tasks are important. But you must know how to prioritize the tasks and allocate your resources to efficiently complete both the tasks in time. You can prioritize based on the importance, the time required, the difficulty, and a number of other criteria. This will help you complete all your tasks efficiently on time.

The Tempting Sorcerer

Distractions derail you from your path. People often focus their energies on unnecessary things like chatting, browsing, etc. when they are supposed to work on an assignment. You spend a lot of time performing unwanted tasks and end up compromising on your productivity. Avoid distractions and keep moving toward your goal.

Um, Tomorrow?

Enough has been said about procrastination in the previous chapter. It is a major hindrance to your progress and you must immediately take notice of it and stop it. Engage in positive procrastination and concentrate on the task to manage your time effectively and attain your goals.

The "No" Problem

Many people have a problem saying "No" to others. They cannot refuse anything and end up with more assignments than they can handle. Another situation is when people have a problem trusting others. They insist on doing everything by themselves and end up with a pile of work and no time. Such people need to be proactive and only accept work that can practically be completed in the stipulate time.

One man cannot do all the work in the world. It needs to be delegated. This often is a problem in an office. This situation affects people and their work-life balance. They cannot concentrate on all types of goals at once and end up being depressed.

Busy Bee

People like to consider themselves as being busy. They like the rush of being occupied and chasing deadlines. They will take up unnecessary work and rush toward the main task with little time on hand. They like the adrenaline rush associated with the process. When this theory goes wrong, it stings pretty badly.

Multitasking is a huge deterrent when it comes to achieving goals.

One at a Time

If you are a juggler, then you are better off in a circus. Multitasking is a huge deterrent when it comes to achieving goals. People consider themselves productive when they are multitasking. What they fail to consider is that they are compromising on the quality of their work. When you answer phone calls, write emails, think about planning your child's birthday, and are upset about being late all at once, how is it going to help your cause?

B-R-E-A-K

Breaks provide you with a breather. They ensure that your mind relaxes so that you can come back strongly and pursue your goals. People fail at time management because they do not balance the break time. They take either long breaks or very short ones. A break should be long enough to rejuvenate you and short enough to help you complete your work in time.

Knowing Thyself

Certain people prefer to wake up early while certain people work at nights. People fail at their tasks when they do not schedule their work properly. You must understand the time at which your energy levels are high and schedule your tasks at that time so that you can achieve your goal. People end up spending a lot of time when they do not schedule their work properly.

Ensure that you do not succumb to these pitfalls when you are in pursuit of your goals.

THE TIMEKEEPER'S SECRET

Let's see how this doctrine can help you overcome time management pitfalls, schedule better, and make time-bound decisions.

Promise

Schedule a goal only when you are committed to it. Be practical and think whether you are going to give a hundred percent to the task. Including a task in your schedule and then falling short of it leads to frustration. It will also affect your other tasks. Preparing and sticking to your schedule is the most important aspect of effective time management.

All Work and No Play

Excelling in just one field of your life is not enough. You need to be proportionate in your success. Every type of goal needs your attention, and dedicating ample time to meet each goal is extremely important. Commitment to fun is as important as commitment to work.

Step by Step

Think about your day in terms of the time in hand and not the task. Once you divide the day into sessions, you can then allocate each session to the task. In that way, you will be able to work, rest, review, and plan at frequent intervals. It is hard to predict the exact time taken to achieve a goal; hence, this method will allow you to change your tactics accordingly.

Focus

Focus on one task at a time. When you focus on a particular task, all your energy is centered on thinking about accomplishing it. Your conscious as well as subconscious mind will think about it all the time and provide you with ways and means to reach your goal. When you multitask or switch between one activity and the other, your mind takes time to adjust to the new activity. Valuable time and energy is lost when this switching takes place on a continuous basis.

Blocks of Time

Analyze your day, week, month, and year according to your plan and allocate a particular block of time for a particular type of goal. For example, you can dedicate weekends for your wife and kids, allocate each morning for your personal wellbeing, and plan a vacation every six months.

Habit

When you remove an H from *habit*, "a bit" remains; when you remove an A from *a bit*, "bit" remains; and when you remove B from *bit*, "it" still remains. Repetition conditions our mind to get used to the task. Engage yourself in a routine and come closer to your goal.

Numero Uno

Finish the prime activity first. Ensure that you schedule your crucial goals first, so that you can finish them at the earliest. Unforeseen circumstances can force you to change your course, so make sure that you finish the important task before it gets interrupted.

Buffer

Schedule a buffer as well. Like mentioned in the earlier point, unforeseen circumstances can occur at any time. Keeping a buffer will act as a cushion when it comes to adjusting your schedule. When things go smoothly, use the buffer time to meet your recreation goals.

Battle the Brain

Battle your brain when it tries to trick you. It will play a lot of mind games and provide you with justifications in order to change your direction and focus. Respond to such situations wisely and remember what is important to you and do it on a priority basis.

Alarm Clock

Set reminders for your tasks. Tell friends and family about your immediate goals. Write them down and place them in prominent locations in your house and workspace. They will constantly remind you about your goal and keep you on track.

Use the effective time management techniques to stay organized and proactive whenever you feel like you are going off track.

THE MULTITASKING MYTH

People generally associate multitasking with efficient time management. It is a myth. It can only be true when the quality aspect is not taken into consideration. But such a thing rarely happens. Quality is a determining factor in every task. Multitasking affects productivity. It might save time initially, but in the long run you will lose a lot of time rectifying qualitative errors.

We think that we can focus on more than one task at a time but we are wrong. When the tasks are of a conflicting nature, our mind gets overloaded. While multitasking, we may think we are focusing on three tasks at once. However, when we focus on those tasks individually, we will be able to finish the task in less time. When we switch between tasks, our mind takes time to adjust. We lose valuable time in the process. When we switch between technical or complex tasks, we lose more time. This activity affects our stress levels as well, and at the end of it we feel drained.

Concentrate on a particular task and you can do more, feel less stressed, and have more energy at the end of the day.

On the contrary, when we focus on a particular task at a time, we tend to be more focused and satisfied. When you feel too stressed concentrating on the same goals for a while, take a breather, refresh yourself, and concentrate on finishing the task. By avoiding multitasking and concentrating on a particular task, you do more, feel less stressed, and have more energy at the end of the day.

Aptitude Effect

The root cause of success is often referred to as aptitude. Aptitude is defined as your ability to do something. People often relate intelligence with grades, but that may not be true always. Intelligence and aptitude are not defined by your grades. They are defined by what you have achieved. Success depends on your aptitude that allows you to take the necessary course of action in order to reach your goals.

You may have a lot of academic degrees, but they are of no use if you do not apply the knowledge that you have gained. Intelligence is acting upon something. You realize your potential only when you make an effort to move in the intended direction. Do not restrict yourself because of your grades or by what anyone else thinks of you. Your aptitude will decide what you are capable of. Manage your time effectively to realize your potential.

Respond vs. React

Do not just react to challenges; respond to them. Take a moment to think and then act. You can react instantly, but you can respond only with a plan. Distinguish between urgent and important tasks. Urgent tasks need immediate attention, whereas important tasks may be related to your long-term plans. Respond cleverly to the tasks that are urgent as well as important. Do not waste your time on tasks that are neither urgent nor important.

The consequences attached to the goal will determine its importance. If a particular task has a great impact on the result, then it is of great significance. Such tasks need to be completed earliest. Tasks that do not have a direct impact on the result can be postponed. Time management teaches you to concentrate on activities that have great consequences to your goal.

Opportunity Cost

Whenever you engage in a particular task, you are missing out on the other one. The opportunity lost is your opportunity cost. Whenever you are performing an activity that is going to take you closer to your goal, think about the opportunity cost. If the opportunity cost of the activities that you have missed is higher, then you need to switch.

Whenever you are watching television, you are not doing something productive and neither will it take you to your goal, so the opportunity cost is high. When you are watching a television show that is related to your goal, then your opportunity cost is low.

Value of the Mysterious Zero

Effective time management involves performing activities that add value. Whenever you are engaged in an activity, ask yourself if that activity is going to contribute to achieving your goal. When you ask this question throughout the day, you will spend less time doing mundane but necessary activities and spend most of your day on performing tasks that will take you closer to your goal. By asking this simple question you will see a dramatic rise in your productivity. You will reach your goals faster.

An old quality management consultant was asked to visit a manufacturing company to inspect and advise on their general operating efficiency. He reached the dilapidated building and surveyed the entire facility. He stumbled upon productivity reports that were photocopied innumerable times from the master copy. The borders of the report were not clear and the heading at the top right- hand corner could not be read. The only thing that was visible was a mysterious zero.

The inspector was curious about the mysterious zero so he checked every document. The zero was printed on every document. He asked people who prepared the reports about the relevance of the zero, but they were clueless about it.

The employees said that they always added a zero at the top right section but they were not aware why. They always did it that way. The consultant was even more intrigued and went to the back office to check the archives. He found records that went back twenty years. The heading was missing but the zero was still there.

He was dejected and was about to leave when a box caught his attention. He went toward it and found out that it contained the master copy. He frantically searched for the heading. The zero was there but this time it was accompanied by the heading, "Number of air strikes today"!

Do you find yourself devoting time to tasks without knowing their relevance? It is time to change.

Do you find yourself devoting time to tasks without knowing their relevance? If yes, then it is time to change. Start asking questions. Solve the mysterious zero story at every stage in your journey toward your goal. In that way, you will manage time effectively and efficiently.

CHAPTER REWIND
CHAPTER REWIND

- If you are a juggler, then you are better off in a circus.

- A break should be long enough to rejuvenate you and short enough to help you complete your work in time.

- Preparing and sticking to your schedule is the most important aspect of effective time management.

- Commitment to fun is as important as commitment to work.

- Once you divide the day into sessions, you can then allocate each session to the task.

- Keeping a buffer will act as a cushion when it comes to adjusting your schedule.

- Take a moment to think and then act.

Chapter 6

BACK IT UP!

*"Give me six hours to chop down a
tree and I will spend the first four
hours sharpening the axe."*
—ABRAHAM LINCOLN

MISS BEAUTY PAGEANT

Tara Conner is a model and Miss USA 2006. Ever
since Tara Conner was a child, her dream was to become a
beauty queen. She won smaller competitions and went on
to compete at the state-level pageantry. You might imagine
she won the state-level competition and went on to become
Miss USA easily. No.

She did not win the state-level beauty pageant; she was
awarded a runner-up prize. This meant that she could not
go to the Miss Universe stage. But her goal was to reach
the ultimate level. Winning and losing Miss Universe

didn't matter, but reaching that stage was her goal. She gathered herself and again contested for Miss Kentucky. For the second time, she was adjudged as a runner-up and not the winner. At that time, her goal seemed very distant. She had two options—forget about it, or make a Plan B.

She wanted to give it one more shot. She was so possessed by her dream that she went to the nearby DVD store and purchased all the DVDs of the Miss Universe beauty pageant. She studied the behavior and the body language of all the contestants who had made it to that level. She absorbed all she could and competed with a renewed spirit. She not only became Miss Kentucky and Miss USA, but also went on to represent her country at the world level. She was among the top five contestants of Miss Universe 2006.

Sometimes, things do not go as planned. In such cases, we have to look at alternatives.

Sometimes, things do not go as planned. In such cases, we have to look at alternatives. We don't have to substitute our goals, but only change the path to reach our goals. When our initial plan does not work out, it is important to have a backup plan, a Plan B, in place.

PLAN B

Just as backup dancers provide support to the main dancer, backup plans support us in the pursuit of our goal. They allow us to remain stress-free and calm when things do not go as planned. When we make an action plan to meet our goals, we do not plan to get fired, meet with an accident, fall ill, etc. Sometimes bad things happen, and we do not have any control over them.

With a backup plan, we can have damage control measures in place. We need to be prepared for the possibility that things may not go according to the plan. Preparing a Plan B will lend us the much-needed support in case of an adversity.

THE WORLD AGAINST YOU

Traditional planning is rigid. It does not anticipate the future challenges. The traditional approach considers the situation to be the same five years down the line. Maybe that system was applicable for previous generations. In today's world, however, we need to be dynamic when we set our goals. The world is changing, and changing rapidly.

Change continues to happen at a brisk pace in every field of life. Be it politics, technology, business, economy, sports, or any other field, change is inevitable. Change can have a positive as well as a negative effect. We can adapt to change and grow, or resist change and remain stagnant. Sometimes, change takes place overnight and we are not left with any options. When such rapid changes take place, backup plans help us stay on the right track. They help us cope up with the change and keep our goals in focus.

TRENDING TRENDS

Large organizations practice strategic planning that involves studying trends in their industry, predicting the patterns, and analyzing the internal and external environment to create foolproof plans. Strategic planning helps organizations to adapt to the change in their environment. We can also adopt strategic or scenario planning when we pursue our goals. Like a company performs scenario analysis, we can also analyze our external and internal environment, anticipate changes, and make backup plans. Scenarios change overnight, but we can be prepared for them by making a good Plan B.

Plan B should be as good as Plan A, so that we can reach our goal with the same intensity with which we had planned. Many wars have been won because of scenario planning. Managers of major companies use this technique to stay ahead of their competition. Scenario planning not only helps you make a Plan B but also create multiple plans like Plan C and Plan D by predicting varied scenarios. By analyzing the past and the present scenario, you can predict the future scenario and plan accordingly to adjust to changes.

When there is no backup plan, adversities can have a huge impact. With nothing to fall back on, we may feel disoriented and depressed and we might lose the energy to pursue our goals. Scenario planning will help us always stay ahead in the game. We will never lose track of our goals with this approach. We will have a plan in place for any kind of adversity. We will just have to reorient ourselves and continue working toward our goal.

NUMBER GAME

Very often people fall prey to the number game. They set the goal to become number one. Being number one is a good thing, but we must consider the cost as well. Being the number one at something by compromising on the quality will not be fruitful in the long run. If a young, newly established company sets its goal to be the leading company of a given field within a year, it is an unrealistic goal. The company will fall short of its goals and get frustrated. Instead, if the company focuses on quality, has a Plan B for possible barriers, and sets its goal to be the number one in the industry in ten years' time, it seems possible.

V FOR VENGEANCE

Give your hundred percent to every task. If your initial plan fails for any reason, make sure you continue working toward your goal with the same intensity. You can only rely on your performance, as it is the only thing in your control. You cannot control the outcome, but you can control how you approach a situation and how much you put in. Just because it's Plan B, that does not mean you can make less effort. In fact, Plan B should motivate you to perform better as you are going toward your goal with a vengeance this time around.

Just because it's Plan B, that does not mean you can make less effort.

GOD'S DREAMS

Sachin Tendulkar is considered to be the "god of cricket." He was inspired to play cricket in 1983 when India won the cricket World Cup. He dreamt of playing for India and winning a world cup. He accomplished his goal of playing for India in the year 1989. He was always a good player and had the potential to be the greatest. He tasted individual success, but the World Cup eluded him for a long while.

He was at his peak in the 1990s, but the team wasn't strong enough to support him. The great man continued playing marvelous innings and kept raising the bar. India came close to victory in the 1996 World Cup, but they lost in the semifinals. The World Cup was lost again. He never gave up and continued playing well. He planned his innings along the way and targeted specific bowlers. He always had a Plan B in place for every situation, but the team failed to execute those plans.

In 2003, India had an inspiring captain and technically advanced support staff. They shared a common goal, but again felt short of winning in the 2003 World Cup Finals.

India hosted the World Cup in 2011. His role had changed from the 1996 World Cup to the 2011 World Cup. He made plans and backup plans and ensured that they worked with a focus on performance. Eventually, his hard work and determination paid off when India won the One-Day International Cricket World Cup in 2011.

His journey teaches us that there will be setbacks and failures in our pursuit, but what matters are our attitude and our belief in our dreams. We need to have proper plans in place for adversities and continue to work diligently toward those.

JUMPING JACK

Everyone is playing jumping jack in today's competitive world. People are trying to outsmart their competition by engaging in a rat race, but they fail to realize that even if they win the race, they will still be rats. Stay out of it. Do not compare your life with others. Set your own benchmarks and compare your efforts to that. Work on setting and raising the bar each time.

When your competitor is also gunning for your goal, it gets a bit murky. This is where you will require flexibility. Sometimes you will have to react instinctively, and at other times you will have to respond tactfully.

Your competition might be constantly on the look out to throw you off your track. They may make use of technology and information to pull you down. However, you need to focus your energy on your goal instead of building strategies to derail others. When you focus on your goal and create backup plans, you stay ahead of the competition. This way, your competitors will always be on your trail and never in front of you.

EMBRACE FAILURE

It is often said that failure is the stepping stone to success. Accept failure and work on your mistakes. Do not let your ego restrict your progress. People spend a lot of time refusing to accept their mistakes. Everyone is aware of a person's mistakes except himself. When you do not accept your mistakes, you spend a lot of energy covering up.

Acceptance is the first step toward progress. If you refuse to accept that your plan failed, you will continue living in an illusory world. When you acknowledge your failure and accept your mistakes, you will be able to face reality. Failure can teach you what not to do. Even if you fail initially, recognize your mistakes, develop a better plan, and proceed toward your goals. Perfection is a myth and failure is a part of life. We should rise from it and continue our journey toward our goal.

FLEXIBLE AS AN AMOEBA

Adapt to information before it overpowers you. Information is the most perishable item. If not acted upon in time, it becomes obsolete. If the new information may help you reach your goal faster or quickly change your course. It may require certain effort, but eventually you will end up saving a lot of time by quick adaptation.

Information is the most perishable item. If not acted upon in time, it becomes obsolete.

Being flexible and relying on a backup plan will give you the freedom to adapt to the new information. Being rigid will only make you stagnated; it won't take you anywhere. Being flexible will allow you to utilize new information and incorporate it to execute Plan B better than Plan A.

STRIKE WHILE THE IRON IS HOT

Gathering information is not enough. Knowledge needs actions to bear results. One can read hundreds of books, but without acting on the principles mentioned in the books no one can be successful. You need to follow the steps to become successful. Books and lectures can give you the knowledge, but you will have to act upon that knowledge to get results.

You will embark on an exciting journey when you start acting upon the principles laid down by success-ful people. The method is the same—it is time-tested and results-oriented, and all it requires from you is the necessary action. Once you have your Plan B, don't wait for the right time. Start acting on it immediately. If you delay, your Plan B will become as stale as old information.

CORRIDOR PRINCIPLE

Corridor principle states that whenever there is an obstacle, it is accompanied with an opportunity. When you start your journey toward your goal, you are bound to be hit by obstacles. When you concentrate and focus on your task, you can find opportunities in them to accomplish your goal you wouldn't even have thought of. Sometimes, you may figure out a Plan B when you are hit by an obstacle on Plan A. The important thing to notice is that you have to keep going even in the face of obstacles.

New doors may open that might lead you toward your goal. If you apply your mind to it, the new opportunity may take you to new horizons. There will be obstacles, but then there will be newer doors. Eventually, you may end up being in a completely different place from where you began, but you will be successful.

KILL OR BE KILLED

Fear stops us from being proactive and creating backup plans. Fear is so powerful that it defeats us in our mind. It doesn't allow us to act. It kills the idea at its inception. Fear is the cause of anxiety, unhappiness, and stress. Obstacles are a part of our life. We need to accept them instead of resisting them. If we don't kill our fear, it will nip our source of motivation.

Don't fear the obstacles, but look them in the eye and challenge them. Once you accept obstacles as a part of your life, it becomes easy to overcome them. Conquering fear will help you start acting on your backup plans and continue working toward your goal.

Self-confidence will help you practice being courageous. It will allow you to overcome your fear on a consistent basis. Once you practice overcoming fear and obstacles, it will become a habit. Successful people have a habit of overcoming their obstacle. It is natural for them. The first step is the most crucial. Once you garner courage to take the first step, the rest will follow. The first step toward your goal often involves a leap of faith.

Believe in yourself. Your self-confidence will help you approach your Plan B with renewed energy and passion and ultimately reach your goal.

HE WHO NEVER THROWS A DICE WILL NEVER GET A SIX

Successful people are risk-takers. They rise above their zone of comfort and are ready to face the consequences. A sound Plan B allows them to take risks. Fearful thoughts are bound to be there; your attitude will decide how well you conquer them. Once you take risks and overcome obstacles, you will not be afraid to take more risks. Risk and return go in proportion. The higher the risk, the higher the return; plan meticulously and do not be afraid to take risks.

AGAIN AND AGAIN UNTIL SUCCESS

When you persist, you develop self-discipline and power. Persistence gives you the power to emerge as a winner against all odds. If you keep persisting, you are bound to get a breakthrough. Every successful person has come across adversity in one form or the other. Persistence is what will keep you upbeat and optimistic about your success.

Problems may knock you down, but persistence will give you the strength to get up and fight back. Accept the fact that you are going to hit a roadblock. To stay persistent on your goal, you have to rise above your barrier and come up with new or improved backup plans. Persistence will take you through your hard times and help you focus on your backup plans.

SHARK TALE

The Japanese have always loved eating fish. But their coastline did not support fishing for decades. Fishermen had to travel a long distance in the sea to catch fish. Due to the distance they used to travel, it took them a long time to come back from the sea. As a result, the fish lost their fresh taste.

The Japanese people could easily make out the taste of stale fish, and the sales declined. To avoid this problem, companies installed freezers on the ships to keep the fish fresh. Freezers allowed the boat to travel further in the sea and stay at sea for a long time. However, the people were not satisfied with the taste of frozen fish either.

Fishing companies installed fish tanks on ships to solve this problem. The fish stayed active for a while in the tank, but they got sluggish in the end. The Japanese people were not satisfied by this either.

The fishing companies finally solved this problem by placing baby sharks in the fish tanks. In this way, the fish remained active and the Japanese people got to taste fresh fish. The fishing industry is huge and many livelihoods are attached to it. When all their plans failed, they did not feel dejected and drop their goal of bringing fresh fish to people. Instead, the fishing companies adopted backup plans at many levels, safeguarded the livelihoods dependent on them, and satisfied all the parties involved.

CHAPTER REWIND
CHAPTER REWIND

- Like a company performs scenario analysis, we can also analyze our external and internal environment, anticipate changes, and make backup plans.

- Right information at the right time can propel you toward your goal.

- People are trying to outsmart their competition by engaging in a rat race, but they fail to realize that even if they win the race they will still be rats.

- Failure can teach you what not to do.

- Reading hundreds of books without acting on the principles mentioned cannot lead to success.

- Don't fear the obstacles, but look them in the eye and challenge them.

- The first step toward your goal often involves a leap of faith.

Chapter 7

MIND GAMES

*"Obstacles are those frightful things you
see when you take your eyes off your goal."*
—HENRY FORD

THE HOUSE OF A THOUSAND MIRRORS

Once upon a time, there was a small village in a land far
away. It was known for its happy and satisfied people. The
village also had a magical place called the "house of a thousand mirrors." One day, a small puppy overheard someone
talking about this place. The dog was fascinated by the idea
of a magical place, so he ventured toward it.

He somehow managed to follow directions and reach
the farmhouse that housed the magical room. The dog was
ecstatic and ran swiftly toward the room. He bubbled with
excitement as he climbed the stairs and reached the room.

When he finally reached the room, he couldn't control his excitement. He entered the room with a beaming face, high-held ears, and a wagging tail. He was surprised to see a thousand happy, smiling faces stare back at him. Their ears were also held high and their tails were also wagging. His joy multiplied when he saw this amazing view. He left the house and promised himself that he would come here very often. The little puppy shared his experience with his friend and suggested he visit the place as well.

The other dog was a little skeptical about this place. He had his reservations but still managed to go to the house of a thousand mirrors. He reached the house and climbed the stairs with an apprehensive look. He hung his head low and opened the door. He was shocked to see a thousand depressed dogs staring at him. He got scared and growled at them and the thousand dogs growled back at him. He left the place and promised himself never to return to this place.

Our mind has a great impact on us. Psychology defines our way of living. Positive thinking can do wonders for you, whereas a negative attitude will convert a rainbow into a colorless object. Psychology has a great impact on the way we visualize our goals and move forward to attain them.

Our mind has a great impact on us. Psychology defines our way of living.

Goal Setting Theory

Goal setting theory was formulated keeping in mind the key principles of psychology and motivation. Goals must be clear and challenging, with achievement as the final payoff. They must also incorporate a feedback mechanism to track your progress. The goal setting theory is a proven theory that describes the implications of setting goals that serve to motivate effectively.

Shine Your Windshield

Just as the windshield should be sparkly clean for a safe drive, there should be clarity in defining your progress and achievement. You should not only know exactly what you want but also know at which stage you are in the pursuit of your goal. Goals that lack clarity guide you in a different direction. Goal setting theory suggests that your goals must be clear so that you can monitor your progress and modify your action plans accordingly.

The Bucket and the Ball

A psychological study was conducted in which people were asked to throw a ball into a bucket from whichever distance they found probable. After a few attempts, people began to judge their capabilities and chose a distance that was neither too close nor too far. Your goals shouldn't be too easy or too tough.

Win-Win Game

Feedback allows you to analyze your strengths and weaknesses. It is important to both give and ask for feedback.

Constructive feedback, positive or negative, motivates you toward your goal. Positive feedback assures that you are on the right track, whereas negative feedback prompts you to work hard before it's too late.

Goals and Clocks

Time and resources need to be allocated with the complexity of the goal in mind. If the goal is too complex and you assign a limited amount of time to it, it is not going to materialize. Similarly, if you assign too much time for a simple task, you are not realizing your potential. We need time to learn and practice complicated tasks. Once we invest in practicing, it will help us in the long run by saving both time and effort.

Seasonal Goals and Life Goals

Athletes frame two sets of goals—one for the season and one for the long run. They set their seasonal goals a notch higher than their previous best and determine the goals for the long run accordingly. If they fail to reach their peak in the current season, they reduce their goals for the current season but compensate by increasing their goals for the long run. We have to evaluate our short-term and long-term goals according to our current performance and make necessary changes to our plans.

Learning as a Goal

Learning goals help us improve our planning, monitoring, and evaluating abilities. When we set smart learning goals to accompany our main goals, they help us focus on developing the skills required to reach our main goal. When we learn new skills, we improve our self-worth and ultimately reach our goal in the process.

Playing with Perception

Psychologists use a technique called *framing* to explain the power of perception. Psychological research found out that people who were made to perceive a task as a threat performed badly at it, but when people were made to perceive the same task as a challenge they excelled at it. Your perception of your goals has a significant impact on how you approach them.

Domino Effect

Success or failure relating to one type of goal has a profound impact on the other types of goals. When your financial goals are not met, your recreational goals are going to suffer. Such a situation can lead to frustration and depression. It is essential to maintain a balance in a crisis, and not let the success or failure of a particular goal affect the other at a major level.

GOAL SETTING THEORY UNDER A MAGNIFYING GLASS

Psychology plays a huge role in determining whether you achieve your goal or not. Your mindset will decide if you are motivated enough to work toward your goals. The goal setting theory establishes the connection between psychology, motivation, and goals. The key findings of this theory provide insights that will help you achieve your goals:

1. Difficulty level of a goal and the sense of achievement are correlated. The higher the difficulty level, the higher the degree of achievement. This finding is based on the assumption that you have the knowledge and the ability to achieve your goal.

2. You can easily monitor performance when your goal is specific. By quantifying or enumerating your goal, you can reduce its variance and gain control over it.

3. The more specific and difficult your goal, the higher the level of performance. When you have vague goals, you cannot perform to the best of your abilities.

Your mindset will decide if you are motivated enough to work toward your goals.

4. When you are dealing with specific and difficult goals, it is extremely important to stay committed. When the difficulty of your goals increases, high commitment level will allow you to stay focused and help you follow your goals.

5. Commitment to a goal can increase when an individual is convinced that the goal is important

and attainable. Here the question of self-efficacy comes into the picture. You can inculcate commitment by adjusting your goals to your capabilities and learning the relevant skills through effective training and experience.

6. Positive feedback encourages you to move toward your goal with more determination. It is instrumental in confirming that you are on the right track and you can concentrate on the same path to achieve your goals.

7. Goal setting and self-efficacy go hand in hand. When individuals find their self-worth to be high, they set higher goals. Self-efficacy also helps to deal with negative feedback or failure. When people crumble under negative feedback or temporary failure, they reduce the intensity level of their goal. If your self-efficacy is high, it will not let criticism bother you.

8. Your goals affect the degree and the direction of your efforts. If a person wants to become a good salesman, he needs to learn the basics of sales, then gain knowledge about the product he would be selling and learn about his competitors. Only then will he be able to formulate a strategy to reach his goal. You have to develop an action plan and put in efforts according to your goals to make sure you reach them.

9. When you constantly keep thinking about your goals, you force your subconscious mind to chalk out a plan to reach there. Even when an obstacle hits you, your mind would find ways and means to get out of it because of your thinking pattern.

10. When you are forced to attain your goal in an unreasonable time frame, you will not be able to give a hundred percent. Your efforts become least effective when you do not possess the relevant skills to absorb the time pressure.

11. Goals serve as standards of self-satisfaction. Attainment of higher goals leads to a higher level of self-satisfaction.

DO YOU SEE SUPERMAN?

A nine-year-old son greeted his father with great enthusiasm when he came back from work. The father was tired and wanted to relax for a while after a hard day's work. The young chap insisted his father play with him in spite of many refusals.

The youngster wanted to spend some quality time with his father, so he kept urging him to play with him. After a while, the father thought of an idea to keep his son engaged. He asked his son to bring a world map. His son obliged. The father told his son that they would be playing a new game today. He tore the world map into pieces and asked his son to reconstruct it. He went to sleep thinking that his son would take a lot of time to complete his task.

The son woke his father in only a few minutes, as he had finished reassembling the map. His father was astonished at his son's achievement. He asked his son how he managed to reconstruct the map within such a short time. His son joyfully replied that on the back of the map there was a picture of Superman. He merely reconstructed Superman and the map automatically reassembled.

Perceiving our goals in a different way can help us simplify things and find innovative solutions. You are capable of doing great things; the only question is, "Are you willing to do them?" Do you get bogged down by the complexity of your goal, or do you see Superman?

Perceiving our goals in a different way can help us simplify things and find innovative solutions.

JOURNALIST AND THE BISCUIT FACTORY

Once, a journalist went to a biscuit factory to interview the owner. As the interview was a standard one, with questions on motivation and the like, the journalist finished the interview in no time. While leaving, he came across a woman who was working in the product line. He thought it would be interesting to get a different perspective, so he decided to ask her a few questions. The woman was very cheerful and greeted him with a smile. She responded to his questions politely. The interview went something like this:

"Since when have you been working here?"

"I started working in the biscuit factory after completing my basic education. It has been fifteen years now that I have been working in the production line."

"What does your job involve? What do you do on a normal day?

"I take packets of biscuits from the conveyer belt and put them in the cardboard boxes."

"So, have you always worked in the production line since you joined? Has your job routine been the same for fifteen years?" asked the journalist, a little perplexed and a little astonished.

The woman smiled and answered in the affirmative. The journalist couldn't help it, and asked her if she didn't find her job a bit boring sometimes.

She dismissed this and said, "I never get bored. Sometimes, they even change the biscuits."

This story teaches us that different things motivate people differently. It is not necessary that what motivates you will motivate someone else. It is therefore important to find what motivates you and leverage it to achieve your goals.

It is important to find what motivates you and leverage it to achieve your goals.

BEING MOTIVATED

Motivation is necessary for a goal-oriented life. It inspires us to act and keep moving toward our goal. Motivation is a process that involves biological, emotional, social, and cognitive forces. It is the result of external and internal factors that stimulate desire and energy in people to achieve their goals. It is a result of conscious and subconscious factors. Our desires, rewards, and expectations form the base of motivation. So, how do you stay motivated?

On and On

Motivation is a continuous phenomenon. You have to stay motivated and do things that motivate you constantly. If you do it only once, you will end up achieving just one goal. In order to achieve all your goals, you will have to stay motivated. You cannot own motivation by practicing it once.

The "You" Power

Motivation is an intrinsic quality. You have to search for it inside yourself. Your will has to fuel your willpower with the right kind of motivation to achieve your goal.

You can become motivated by listening to others' ideas, but at the end of the day what motivates others may not motivate you. You have to find out what motivates you. Motivation is an individualistic trait. You have to practice it individually to perfect it. You will have to motivate yourself until the time you start doing it naturally.

You are bound to make mistakes along the road, but it is important to stay motivated, learn from those mistakes, and move forward. Believe in yourself; if you do not have faith in yourself, no one will. Once you excel at the art of motivation, you may not need to consciously spend time to motivate yourself; your subconscious mind will motivate you automatically.

One More Time

You always have a choice to be motivated or be depressed. Our greatest weakness lies in giving up. Never give up. The most certain way to succeed is to try one more time. Motivation will allow you to try one more time.

You require motivation the most when you are down and out, not when you are at the top. When you are at the top, you will perform better to stay there, but when you fall you will require the right kind of motivation to pick you up and put you on track. You cannot sit on the fence; you have to make a choice whether you want to get motivated or stay depressed.

Oasis in Sight

Expectancy theory states that people can stay motivated by expecting the outcome of their acts. A reward is an excellent motivator. We work for rewards. When you expect to derive a specific benefit by achieving your goal, you become motivated. You expect a positive outcome from your actions and hope to be rewarded.

F-O-C-U-S

Staying focused is a huge motivational technique. When you start deviating from your goal, use your reward to motivate you to come back on track. If your financial goal is to build a house, then think about the house to stay focused and move toward your goal. It is never late to chase your dreams.

Congratulating Yourself

Keeping records of your progress will help you stay motivated. Your progress will remind you about your successes in the past and motivate you to achieve success in the future as well. Keeping records of your achievements will orient your subconscious mind to think positively.

Antenna for Information

Be receptive to knowledge and criticisms. Reading books and stories is a great way to get motivated. Real life incidents can also stimulate you to think in a positive manner and get motivated to achieve something. At the same time, look for people who indulge in constructive criticism. This will help you look at where you are going wrong and align yourself. All this is only possible if you don't have a closed mindset. Be receptive and gain a lot of knowledge, channel it, and attain your goal.

Contagious

Motivation is contagious. Exposing yourself to highly motivated people will motivate you as well. It plants a seed in your mind that develops over time and germinates into something that you desire to achieve. Staying with people who uplift you will have a positive impact on you and your family members.

Everyone radiates energy, either positive or negative. Motivation feeds on positive energy and spreads rapidly. Negativity can affect it quickly and reduce its impact. Thus, it is important to surround yourself with positivity to stay motivated and pursue your goals.

Bumblebee Argument

There is a popular joke about science and human laws. Scientists opine that the bumblebee has a hefty body. Its wingspan is also very small. Aerodynamically, the bumblebee shouldn't be able to fly. But how does the bumblebee manage to fly, then? It's because it doesn't care for human laws. On a serious note, what the argument suggests is that nothing is impossible and no one can tell you that you cannot achieve something.

Stay motivated, be positive, and keep walking toward your goals; slowly but steadily you will reach them.

CHAPTER REWIND
CHAPTER REWIND

- Time and resources need to be allocated with the complexity of the goal in mind.

- We have to evaluate our short-term and long-term goals according to our current performance and make necessary changes to our plans.

- Your perception of your goal has a significant impact on how you approach it.

- When individuals find their self-worth to be high, they set higher goals.

- When you constantly keep thinking about your goals, you force your subconscious mind to chalk out a plan to reach them.

- You cannot sit on the fence; you have to make a choice whether you want to get motivated or stay depressed.

- Staying with people who uplift you will have a positive impact on you and your family members.

Chapter 8

THE MYSTERIOUS POWER WITHIN YOU

*"The possibilities of creative effort
connected with the subconscious mind
are stupendous and imponderable.
They inspire one with awe."*
—NAPOLEON HILL

JACK AND HIS FRIEND

A sales job is all about meeting targets and goals. A young salesperson named Jack was performing his best and was meeting his monthly targets. He was the best among his peers. One day, Jack's manager called him in and told him that there had been a change in the strategy. He ordered Jack to double his sales for the month.

Jack was performing to his potential and was selling a thousand units per month. Now, with his goal doubled, he would have to sell two thousand units. Jack was very depressed about this farfetched idea and spoke with his friend about it over dinner. His friend was an eternal optimist and encouraged Jack to look at it as a challenge and not as a threat.

Jack's friend advised him to tap into his subconscious and come up with creative solutions. He asked Jack to think about the problem as if his life depended on it. Jack ridiculed the idea at first, but after a lot of convincing his friend set Jack upon an exercise. He asked Jack to come up with ideas while he made a list of them.

Jack came up with a few outrageous ideas at first, but after some time, his thought process became more streamlined. Initially, he told his friend that to achieve his goal he would have to be at two places at once. But as his thought process aligned, he realized that he would have to make multiple presentations and speak to as many clients as possible.

Jack then came up with several productive ideas, like holding a seminar where he could speak with a lot of people at once and explain the benefits of his product over some coffee and donuts. He thought of combining cold calling with his travel time and harnessing the power of social media to further his cause. At the end, when Jack's friend gave him the list, the number of good ideas that he had come up with astonished him. Eventually, he accomplished his goal of selling two thousand units in that month.

We have a tendency to limit ourselves, but our subconscious cannot be caged. Nothing is impossible for our subconscious mind. It is free. All we have to do is channel its power to achieve our goals. Our subconscious mind comes up with solutions when we think hard about our goals. There is an immense amount of power in positive visualization. By tapping our subconscious, we will be able to attract things that will help us reach our goals.

By tapping our subconscious, we will be able to attract things that will help us reach our goals.

TAPPING THE SUBCONSCIOUS

Achievers from different fields have been practicing and continue to practice the art of subconscious goal setting. Athletes, entrepreneurs, politicians, actors, etc. have used this technique to be successful and stay successful. Their goal-oriented journey usually begins with an idea that they implant in their subconscious. The idea possesses them, and thereafter every step that they take is in the direction of their goal. Setting subconscious goals will motivate you to act to your potential and achieve the desired result. To set subconscious goals, you just have to think about them constantly. This will help you focus and make optimal use of your resources to achieve your goal.

You should control your
mind rather than let your
mind control you.

It is extremely important to be the master of your mind. You should control your mind rather than let your mind control you. When you control your mind, you can think positively and eradicate the negative thoughts, but when your mind controls you it clutters your thinking process by creating a dark shadow of negativity.

You can attract wealth and happiness by using your sub-conscious mind. You can fulfil all types of goals by utilizing the law of attraction. The key to the law of attraction is positive thinking. Positive thinking affects your dominant thought process and you start unlocking your potential. You start to discover opportunities that take you closer to your goal. Condition your mind to think positively. When you keep on thinking about your goal, your body, mind, and soul will adapt to it. You will become comfortable with the idea and automatically start moving toward your goal.

THREE MINDS: ID, EGO, AND SUPEREGO

Sigmund Freud's psychoanalytic theory states that the id, ego, and superego are three parts of the human personality. They are also known as our three minds. The id, also known as the subconscious mind, is responsible for meeting our basic needs. It demands instant gratification of our wants and needs. It is a large storehouse of our memories and feelings. It functions autonomically.

The ego represents the conscious mind; it deals with reality. It meets the requirements of the id in an acceptable manner. It rationalizes things and then acts upon them. The ego is that part of the mind that is aware and makes decisions. Its decisions are influenced by the subconscious mind.

The superego is based on morals and judgements dealing with right or wrong. This third dimension is referred to as supra/super-conscious as well. It goes by other names like o*ver soul, collective unconscious, infinite intelligence*, and *god mind*. This universal power has been credited with being responsible for major breakthroughs.

This mysterious power is what enables musicians to create compositions and helps scientists to think of the unthinkable. Extraordinary things are the manifestations of this super-conscious mind. The super-conscious and the subconscious mind prompt the conscious mind to take action on the plan set up by them in order to enable you to reach your goal.

When you zero in on your goal and think about it continuously, you activate your id, ego, and superego and compel them to find solutions and develop a roadmap that will lead you toward your goal. You can get what you want by harnessing the power of these three minds. The only limiting factor in this case is your own imagination.

AWAKENING YOUR SUBCONSCIOUS

Throughout the history of mankind, successful people have activated their subconscious mind and achieved what nobody else could achieve. The secret has been guarded and transferred for ages, but now it is out in the open. The power of the subconscious mind can be utilized by anyone. You possess the power; you just have to activate it. You can get what you want by visualizing it over and over again.

It is said that whatever the human mind can conceive, it can achieve. The solution to a problem begins in the mind but is cluttered with negativity. Humans think negatively by default. You have to clear the clutter with positive thinking. Once you eradicate the negativity, you will be able to see the solutions and opportunities clearly. Your subconscious mind feeds on positivity. Positive thoughts will activate your subconscious and you will see a dramatic change in the way you perceive the world.

Your problems can be solved with sound interaction between your conscious and subconscious minds. By engaging yourself in the following exercise, you will be able to perceive the truth. The first step is to identify your problem; the interaction requires knowing the exact nature of the problem so that your mind can come up with a plausible solution to it. Clearly defining the problem involves writing the problem down or creating a vivid mental picture of the problem. This will lend lot of clarity and your mind will be able to focus on the solutions.

The next step is to accumulate information regarding the problem. You might have faced a similar problem in the past or a friend or a relative might have faced it earlier. By understanding how you or others had overcome the problem, your mind will conclude that the problem can be solved. Your mind will conjure similar solutions by working on the data that you feed it.

Once you present your subconscious mind with a problem, it works continuously to find a solution to it. You may be driving, sleeping, or working, but your subconscious will be thinking of ways to overcome the problem. It makes use of your beliefs and positive thoughts to come up with an answer.

Once you present your subconscious mind with a problem, it works continuously to find a solution to it.

The activated subconscious mind will not stop thinking about a solution until it finds one. Your conscious mind does not need to think about the problem once all the necessary information is provided to the subconscious mind. You can afford to rest and relax; the answer will come to you at the right time.

TRAVEL LIGHT—STOP CARRYING EXTRA BAGGAGE

Change your state of mind and you will be able to achieve all types of goals and lead a balanced life. The key to unlocking the door to a balanced lifestyle lies in your mind. You have to surround yourself with positivity and compel your mind to be in a happy state.

Positivity attracts positivity and negativity attracts negativity. If you think you are incapable of losing weight, you never will be able to lose weight. Negative thoughts regarding your weight will depress you and you will end up piling on more pounds. If you think positively and believe you can lose weight, your mind will curb your desire to eat unhealthy food and order your body to start exercising to lose weight. Successful people attract more success, and unsuccessful people crumble under self-doubt. Start believing in yourself and witness the change.

Get rid of your baggage. Baggage slows you down and does not allow you to climb the stairs of success. You might have failed in the past, but start on a clean slate and be positive. There can be many reasons for your failure in the past. By thinking positively, activating your subconscious mind, channeling the power of visualization, and working hard toward your goal, you are bound to succeed.

Believe in yourself and take the leap of faith. Be truthful to yourself in the process. Accept your mistakes and work toward rectifying them. Your ego will not allow you to grow. Get rid of it. Accept your faults and get rid of the excess baggage that you have been carrying around for years. Start a new life with renewed enthusiasm and be positive.

Every successful plan is executed twice—once in the mind and once in reality. We are what we are because of our thoughts. We have the power to script our future with the help of our thoughts. We have the power to create our own reality. We must train our minds to reject negative thoughts.

A 70-YEAR OLD WOMAN AND HER MEMORY

A 70-year-old woman was known for her strong memory. However, as age caught up with her she began to forget things. She started forgetting dates, faces, common places of things, etc. She developed a habit of saying, "I cannot remember things because of my age. I am losing my memory." She started repeating the sentence umpteen times in a day. She even started using the line at the start of her every conversation.

Someone suggested she stop saying the sentence if she wanted to regain her ability to recall her memory. From that day onward, the old woman resisted the urge to blame her loss of memory on her age. She started saying, "I am in complete control of my memory and remember things vividly."

Over a period, she regained her memory and did not suffer memory lapse. This wasn't any miracle, but the power of suggestion in action. Earlier, she gave her subconscious negative suggestions. But later on, she changed it to positive and benefitted from it. When you suggest to your mind that you are capable of reaching your goals, it accepts the suggestion and works in that fashion. Use the power of suggestion to reach your goals.

DARK AND LIGHT SHADED SUNGLASSES

Humans possess unlimited mental powers. An average person is not aware of this powerhouse and thus leads his life in an average manner. Successful people have unraveled this mystery and have taken giant strides toward their goals. If you wear a dark shade of sunglasses, you will visualize the world as dark, whereas light-shaded sunglasses will present you with a different picture.

Visualization also works in the same manner. You will see the world based on how you visualize it. When you visualize your goal, you will automatically start spotting opportunities that will lead you there. Leaders develop this technique and envision their success. They follow their vision until the time it turns into reality. Throughout history, great leaders have mastered the art of effective visualization.

Visualization is not an alien concept. We visualize all the time. We visualize when we look forward to reaching home after work, we visualize our weekends, etc. You have to channel this vision and think in terms of your goals. Once you practice this technique, your vision will improve and you will be able to see things clearly and, ultimately, your vision will be converted into reality.

Before every important assignment, visualize your success. Football players visualize the way they will score goals the next day before going to sleep. Actors visualize how they are going to perform on a particular scene. Visualization provides you with the confidence that a particular task can be achieved. It tells you that you have already achieved your goal in your head and it is time to achieve it in the practical sense. Unsuccessful people indulge in negative visualization. They see how they failed the last time they performed at a similar task. Negative visualization defeats them in the mind itself.

Live in your dream house and drive your dream car in your head.

Visualize your life as you want it to be. This does not include just wishing for a grand house or driving a sports car. Visualizing includes living the life in your mind. You have to live in your dream house and drive your dream car in your head.

Many people act on impulse and say things they do not mean. Visualizing can help overcome this problem as well. It is a great tool to build character. Visualizing your behavior at a particular event before its occurrence can train your mind to give your body the right impulse. If you are going to a party, visualize yourself at the party speaking with the people. Come across as a calm and composed personality if that is what you want to project. Playing out your actions in the mind will certainly help you be in control of your actions once the real event takes place.

You should visualize often and for long durations. Your visuals should be vivid and intense. You should be emotionally invested in your visualizations. Visualization techniques may not yield results overnight. You have to be patient. You need to work persistently and consistently toward your goal. Visualization will provide you with opportunities, but eventually you will have to make use of those opportunities by performing the required actions.

Practice the visualization technique before going to sleep. Start with visualizing your next day. Think about performing all the productive tasks that will take you closer to your goal. Analyze your tasks once you have performed them. Rectify your mistakes and repeat the visualization process for the next day. Gradually, you can widen the scope of this activity and visualize long-term processes before executing them.

THE MYSTERIOUS SUPER-CONSCIOUS MIND

The super-conscious mind is responsible for generating path-breaking ideas. Innovators have constantly gained a lot from their super-conscious mind. They have achieved their goals by unlocking the power within. The idea and the subsequent process originate in our super-conscious mind.

You can tap into your super-conscious mind when you are in a relaxed state of mind. Your super-conscious mind takes over your thinking when you submit yourself to it.

You will get ideas that will lead you toward your goal when you learn this mysterious way of thinking. Entrepreneurs and artists are known to be creative in their approach to reach their goal. Creative solutions come from within each of us. You just need to channel your thoughts to unleash your creativity. Your super-conscious mind can come up with outside-of-the-box solutions.

Leonardo da Vinci used to make use of the mysterious power of the super-conscious mind. He would sit at his desk leisurely and dive deep into his consciousness. He used to close his eyes, relax his body and mind, and scribble whatever thoughts came to his mind on a writing pad. Once done with this exercise, he used to search for patterns in the random designs he created on the paper. He used his super-conscious mind to bring ideas to the surface. Many of his inventions were a result of this method.

When you visualize with right emotions in a relaxed atmosphere, your super-conscious mind activates and takes charge of your thinking process. It will present you with an idea at any time. You might connect that thought with the headlines on a news channel or an advertisement on a radio. The super-conscious mind chooses mysterious ways to give us the answer to our problems. Believe in the power of your super-conscious mind, perform the exercise, and wait for the right moment for the answer to appear in front of you.

CHAPTER REWIND
CHAPTER REWIND

- Positive thinking affects your dominant thought process and you start unlocking your potential.

- When you keep on thinking about your goal, your body, mind, and soul will adapt to it.

- Your problems can be solved with sound inter-action between your conscious and subcon-scious minds.

- The key to unlocking the door to a balanced lifestyle lies in your mind.

- Start believing in yourself and witness the change.

- Every successful plan is executed twice—once in the mind and once in reality.

- Before every important assignment, visualize your success.

Chapter 9

THEY HAVE DONE IT, NOW IT'S YOUR TURN

*"The more intensely we feel about an idea
or a goal, the more assuredly the idea,
buried deep in our subconscious, will
direct us along the path to its fulfilment."*
—EARL NIGHTINGALE

Until now, we have seen various models, techniques, and methods that will help you reach your goal. This chapter consists of five inspiring stories—four real-life stories and one based on mythology. These real-life stories will tell you the importance of a goal-oriented approach to life and analyze the power of goals in the life of an individual, a team, an organization, a country, and a god.

INDIVIDUAL: THE PHOENIX NAMED OPRAH WINFREY

Oprah Winfrey is considered one of the most influential people in America and the world. Her journey has been a constant struggle. She has battled all odds to reach where she is now. She is among the richest women in America and the first African-American billionaire. But her journey hasn't been a cakewalk. Her battle with destiny started when she was six years old.

She had moved to Milwaukee to live with her less supportive mother. Their standard of living was poor and the near future had not looked promising. As she grew up, members of her own family sexually harassed her. It shook her. The traumatic experiences distressed her greatly. With no one to lend support, she chose to live in an illusionary world, which she accessed using drugs. Her grief and the incidents that tore her soul drew her to drugs. She turned to a life of rebellion and ended up in numerous juvenile detention centers.

Her father attempted to revive her by imposing strict rules and making education her priority. After the initial push, Oprah realized the value of life and concentrated on her education. Her mindset changed and her life got a purpose. She set smart goals, both short-term and long-term, and started working toward them. From being a wayward individual, she became a goal-oriented student. She became an honors student and received a full scholarship to Tennessee State University. She majored in speech communications and performing arts and regained her confidence. Education provided her self-belief and motivated her to set higher goals in life.

Her meteoric rise began when she oriented her life toward her goals. At the age of 18, she won a beauty pageant. Later, she became the youngest news anchor. Due to the excellent control and intelligence she displayed, she was promoted as the co-host for a local talk show called *People Are Talking*. After her involvement, the show's popularity escalated. She was given control of the show and it was renamed as *The Oprah Winfrey Show*.

Her talk show became a phenomenon all over the world. She became a household name, and then there was no looking back. She capitalized on her brand name and started her own production house, Harpo Productions. She launched Oprah.com and subsequently started a cable channel and a magazine. She always worked toward being significant, and success followed her.

Oprah faced various challenges throughout her life. She started setting well-defined goals and overcame her challenges one by one. If she had not envisioned her success, she could not have reached it. Every time adversity hit her, she rose from the ashes like a phoenix. Oprah Winfrey followed her goals and became one of the most influential people in America.

Oprah spotted opportunities because she was looking for them. Sometimes, you will be able to easily spot opportunities. But there will also be times when you will be down and out. Opportunities will still be there, but if you don't explore them they will pass you by.

We get what we ask for in life.

Oprah had the hunger to succeed. She planned at every stage and set goals accordingly. Her goals changed, but her approach remained the same. Her life story teaches us that there is no substitute for hard work. We get in life what we ask for. Her often-repeated quote is, "The right to choose your own path is a sacred privilege; use it wisely." Set smart goals for yourself and get motivated to achieve what you always wanted.

TEAM: MIRACLE MEN IN BLUE

Goals are not necessarily individual in nature. Sometimes, a group of people share the same goals and have to work in unison to achieve those goals. This type of behavior is common in sports teams. Cricket is considered a religion in India, and this story is about a miracle.

Team India went to the West Indies in the year 2007 with the agenda of winning the One-Day International Cricket World Cup. They had the favorites tag attached to them as the team was filled with star performers. The team that was supposed to win the World Cup failed even to qualify for the second round. They were knocked out and faced a lot of flak from people and the media for their dismal performance.

Twenty 20 (T20) cricket was at a promising stage in 2007, and the Board of Control for Cricket in India (BCCI) wasn't quite supportive of the format. The T20 World Cup was due in months and the board selected a young team with minimal experience to represent the country. No one believed in this team. The fans thought that when a star-studded team could fall like nine pins, this novice team stood no chance.

The players, led by a resilient captain named Mahendra Singh Dhoni, saw this as an opportunity to salvage some pride. They had nothing to lose. They prepared and played hard with the idea of enjoying their game. The tournament kicked off on a negative note as Team India's first match against Scotland was rained out. Due to that, the next match against arch-rival Pakistan became a do-or-die encounter for the team. The match ended in a tie, and eventually India won the game by emerging victorious in the bowl-out that is used to decide a tie match.

They qualified for the next round but lost the match against New Zealand. Again, they were put in a critical situation in the next match against England. It took a once-in-a-lifetime performance from batsman Yuvraj Singh, who smashed six sixes in an over to derail England. They then faced a formidable opponent in South Africa, but man-aged to channel the momentum and won against them as well. India entered the semifinals to face the One-Day International Champions, Australia. India won the game by playing out of their skins and qualified for the finals against Pakistan.

A final match is generally about handling nerves; whichever team handles pressure best wins the tournament. India versus Pakistan generally is a high-octane game, and this was no different. After a roller-coaster ride, the win-lose situation boiled down to the nail-biting last few overs. Pakistan was chasing a target set by India and had a good chance of reaching it.

That was when captain Dhoni took a gamble and asked an inexperienced Joginder Sharma to bowl the last over instead of the seasoned Harbhajan Singh, who was at the receiving end in his last over. A miscued shot by the batsman cost Pakistan the Cup, and India pulled off a miraculous win.

India's journey was filled with obstacles, but they managed to overcome those obstacles and achieved their goal. They planned at each level and executed their strategy to steadily inch closer to the ultimate goal. They faced hiccups as well but regained their composure by reviewing their performance and staying motivated. It took a calculated risk to win the cup and achieve the goal, but their journey was well-planned and backed by performance.

If you analyze the above journey closely, you will find a well-motivated team. It was the feeling of redemption that motivated the team. They set their eyes on the trophy but took each game as it came. They planned and modified their strategy for every game. They set individual targets for players, which eventually contributed to the team's success. Their journey wasn't smooth, but the captain made sure that the team enjoyed its journey. The team effectively handled and channeled pressure, which is unavoidable in a sport like cricket. In the end, they managed their resources and delivered a stellar performance to achieve their goal.

Miracles will happen only if you want them to happen.

From Team India's story, you can learn that you should not let any situation overpower you. Remain focused on your goal and give your best performance. There will be setbacks, but you can overcome them if you are motivated to achieve your goal. Miracles will happen only if you want them to happen. Plan meticulously and analyze your every move. Take a step back whenever necessary in order to gain momentum and take the leap to achieve your goal.

ORGANIZATION: WAL-MART'S RETAIL THERAPY

Organizations are goal-oriented entities that follow a combination of techniques to achieve their goals. They have a clear vision and mission to reach their goals. Managers follow a strategy that leads the employees toward their goals and the organization toward theirs. All of us know Wal-Mart. But how did they start? Let us look at the goals Wal-Mart had for itself when it started.

Wal-Mart is the world's largest retailer and an economic force to reckon with. Wal-Mart has become a giant with a global impact. But when Sam Walton founded Wal-Mart, his goal was to provide shoppers products at lower prices than were available anywhere else. The entire business strategy was, and still is, centered on this goal. Providing goods at the lowest price is easier said than done. However, Wal-Mart has consistently managed to achieve their goal.

Wal-Mart started functioning in the early 1960s. Even though the goal was daunting, their plan to achieve it was simple. Sam Walton wanted to offer goods at the cheapest price without concentrating on the margins. He dealt in volume. The low prices attracted a lot of people. The company continued to grow and went public in the year 1970. It added store after store and surpassed its competitors.

Wal-Mart's philosophy was to keep expenses to the bare minimum. Sam Walton, despite being the founder, travelled modestly and shared rooms with colleagues on business trips. The organization took every step keeping in mind its core strategy of being cost effective. Sam Walton died in 1992, but his organization continues to follow his strategy.

Today, Wal-Mart is exploring new avenues by venturing into new countries every year. It finds novel ways to grow and offer more products and services to its customers.

They continue to expand by following their central policy of keeping prices low. They have amalgamated the technology and corporate culture into their low-cost policy. They manage to keep their prices low by employing cutting-edge technology, economical corporate culture, and powerful negotiations with the suppliers to sell merchandise at cheaper rates. Their strategic alliances also serve their ultimate goal of delivering the goods at the lowest possible prices.

Wal-Mart teaches us the value of goals. It teaches us to align our approach, keeping in mind the focal point of our goal. It takes courage to envision an empire. If Sam Walton had not envisioned Wal-Mart, the gargantuan organization would not have materialized. It is important to dream and convert it into reality by setting goals and relentlessly working toward achieving them. Wal-Mart set goals all the way from the foundation to the top. At all levels, the employees have clear-cut roles and responsibilities. The management constantly works to introduce innovative ideas.

When you plan with determination and persistence to achieve your goal, no goal is impossible.

Wal-Mart planned its success by setting strategic short-term and long-term goals. They never compromised on their core objective of providing goods at the cheapest rate at any stage. Similarly, your every move should be goal-directed. Your thought process should be goal-oriented and embedded in every person's mind associated with the goal. Every spoke of the wheel should be aligned to the goal. When you plan with determination and persistence to achieve your goal, no goal is impossible.

COUNTRY: RESURRECTION OF THE LAND OF THE RISING SUN

Japan, as it is known today, is a developed country and a frontier in technology. But when Japan was severely hit during the Second World War, it was a crippled nation. Japan lost its manpower and a quarter of its wealth. One week after atomic bombs had obliterated the cities of Hiroshima and Nagasaki, emperor Hirohito spoke directly to his subjects through a four-minute radio address. The historic address ended the war and triggered Japan's rise from the ashes. He urged the citizens to surrender and ended his speech by advising Japanese people to cultivate the ways of rectitude, foster nobility of spirit, and work with resolution to keep pace with the progress of the world. He asked his fellow citizens to endure the unendurable and suffer the insufferable.

After the war, the Japanese government began its resurrection. They promoted specific industries and discouraged foreign and domestic competition. They created informal trade barriers to protect their economy from competition. Their plans focused on higher saving rates and lowering the inflation. America also purchased a lot of goods and services from Japan. Later on, free trade policies created a favorable situation for Japanese exports.

Japan changed its industry setup by concentrating on goods that did not require many imports. Earlier they were dependent on imported raw material, but with a shift in policy they started making goods like cars that did not require many imports. They strengthened their economy by exporting.

They focused on educating the youth. They fostered industrial unions that led to sound cooperation between workers and management. Major industries offered life-time employment. They rewarded loyalty and compensated employees handsomely when they remained with the organization for a long time. The voters chose the Liberal Democratic Party. They invested their faith in one party for years that ensured a stable political situation.

The United States viewed Japan as a strategic ally during the Cold War and took care of its defense requirements. As a result, Japan did not invest much in raising their own army and concentrated on other sectors. The Japanese economy has been stagnant in recent decades, but its meteoric rise after the catastrophic bombings is indeed commendable. Japan also has a history with earthquakes and seismic activity as it is located near major tectonic plate boundaries. Time and again, the country has shown great determination to battle manmade and natural disasters.

Japan followed a goal-oriented approach and enjoyed its success. Citizens together make a country, and when a country achieves a goal it is because every citizen has performed their role well. Japan had to formulate well-defined short-term, medium-term, and long-term goals to rise above the catastrophe. They had to make sure that progress was made in every sector.

Japan could rise against all odds because, even when it had lost everything, the country did not lose its belief. The citizens of Japan believed that they could achieve their goal. A new Japan was born after the bombings. Just as a newborn has to crawl, toddle, fall, balance, and walk before it starts to run, Japan also had to undergo various phases of development. If the nation had directly set a goal to run, it would've faltered in the process.

Unfaltering focus on goals and unrelenting hard work bring a vision to reality.

A country has to excel in many sectors to develop. Japan set clear goals pertaining to all sectors like politics, industry, society, economy, etc. Every goal was aligned and directed toward success. Japan had a vision and it came true because of its unfaltering focus on its goals and unrelenting hard work.

GOD: THE INDIAN LEGEND OF NARSIMHA AVATAR

Hindu mythology depicts Lord Vishnu as the preserver of the cosmic order. The *asuras* (demons) were known to wreak havoc and create an imbalance. In order to restore the balance, Vishnu had to battle the *asuras*. Every battle involved a different *asura,* and it is said that Vishnu took different avatars to kill each. Hiranyakashipu was one such *asura* who had to face Vishnu's wrath. But conquering Hiranyakashipu was difficult, as he had obtained a boon that made him invincible.

After the death of his younger brother, Hiranyakashipu is said to have performed a ritual penance for which he obtained a boon of his choice. He specifically asked for a boon that entailed that he could be killed neither by a man nor by an animal, neither in the day nor at night, neither inside a residence nor outside it, neither on the ground nor in the sky, and neither with a weapon nor a tool.

Vishnu analyzed the situation and looked at the terms and conditions. At first, the boon seemed foolproof; there was no way Hiranyakashipu could be killed. However, after much deliberation Vishnu looked at the situation intricately and found a solution. To kill this *asura*, Vishnu transformed himself into an avatar called Narsimha. Narsimha was a creature that was part human and part animal. Narsimha caught hold of the *asura* at twilight, which is neither day nor night. He dragged the *asura* to the threshold, which is neither inside a house nor outside, and placed him on his lap, which is neither on the ground nor in the sky. Narsimha eviscerated the *asura* with his sharp claws, which are neither weapons nor tools. Thus, Vishnu was able to rid the world of a demon like Hiranyakashipu.

Even though this is mythology, it is worth noting that Vishnu killed the demon through meticulous evaluation of the situation that enabled him to come up with a plan best suited to achieve the goal.

> **When you apply your mind and focus on your goal, you will find a way.**

In life, you may face many situations that will seem insurmountable at first. However, when you apply your mind to it and focus on your goal, you will find out a way. On looking closely, you will find a path that will eventually take you toward your goal.

Remember, if they can do it, you can do it too.

CHAPTER REWIND
CHAPTER REWIND

- Oprah spotted opportunities because she was looking for them. Sometimes, you will be easily able to spot opportunities. But there will also be times when you will be down and out. Opportunities will still be there, but if you don't explore them, they will pass you by.

- From Team India's story, you can learn that you should not let any situation overpower you. Remain focused on your goal and give your best performance. There will be setbacks, but you can overcome them if you are motivated to achieve your goal. Miracles will happen only if you want them to happen. Plan meticulously and analyze your every move. Take a step back whenever necessary in order to gain momentum and take the leap to achieve your goal.

- Wal-Mart teaches us the value of goals. It teaches us to align our approach keeping in mind the focal point of our goal. It takes courage to envision an empire. If Sam Walton had not envisioned Wal-Mart, the gargantuan organization would not have materialized. It is important to dream and convert it into reality by setting goals and relentlessly working toward achieving them. Wal-Mart set goals all the way from the foundation to the top.

- Japan could rise against all odds because, even when it had lost everything, the country did not lose its belief. The citizens of Japan believed that they could achieve their goal. A new Japan was born after the bombings. Just as a newborn has to crawl, toddle, fall, balance, and walk before it starts to run, Japan also had to undergo various phases of development. If the nation had directly set a goal to run, it would've faltered in the process.

- Vishnu killed the demon through meticulous evaluation of the situation that enabled him to come up with a plan best suited to achieve the goal. In life, you may face many situations that will seem insurmountable at first. However, when you apply your mind to it and focus on your goal, you will find out a way. On looking closely, you will find a path that will eventually take you toward your goal.

Chapter 10

100 Ways to Live

This additional section will enlighten you with 100 ways to live the life of your dreams. The following pointers will help you score goals, stay on the right path, and lead a successful, balanced lifestyle. Read them as often as possible to stay motivated and achieve your goal.

THE CENTURY OF GOALS

1. A blind man may lack eyesight, but even he can have a vision. Draw a vision for yourself and work hard to get there. Set realistic and challenging goals.

2. Absorb all the good qualities from the people you meet. Everyone has positive traits; be sure to make a note of them and incorporate the same in your daily life.

3. Always be thirsty for knowledge. Stay motivated and keep learning and gaining knowledge.

4. Always have an ethical approach toward your goal. Play hard but play fair. Remember that there are no shortcuts to success. Ethical ways will take you to your goal slowly but surely.

5. Always keep your eyes and ears open. We live in the information age. Information is flying in the air; all you have to do is be receptive and capitalize on the information.

6. Always stay calm and composed. It will streamline your thinking and help you make decisions quickly. Do not be disturbed by your internal or external environment.

7. Ask "why" for every act you perform. This will protect you from wasting your time on unproductive activities and thoughts. Your answer to the question will align your actions toward your goals.

8. Ask yourself whether performing a certain task is going to take you closer to your goal or away from it. Focus on tasks that take you closer to your goal and discard those that take you away from it.

9. Avoid extremism and practice moderation. The secret to a successful life is balance. Balance your life by balancing your goals. Concentrate on each type of goal uniformly.

10. Be a leader and carve a way for others to follow. To be a good leader you have to be a good follower. Remember to switch between being a leader and a follower according to the situation.

11.   Be committed to what you do and never give up. Prepare and work hard at every task. Act gracefully under pressure and be known for your character.

12.   Be content with what you have. This does not mean you set few goals. This means that you set goals that will lead to contentment. Do not over-commit to materialistic goals.

13.   Be courteous to others. Greet people with a smile. It radiates positivity and forms a chain that makes many people smile. Communicate effectively to raise the quality of your life.

14.   Be good to people and foster new friendships. Do not develop a relationship with the selfish thought of benefitting from their friendship. Be genuine and you will develop a network, which is neither selfish nor materialistic.

15.   Be patient with your efforts. Success is not an overnight phenomenon. A tree doesn't grow in days; it takes years to grow. Keep walking, and slowly and steadily you will reach your destination.

16.   Be punctual; it shows that you respect time. A punctual person respects his own time as well as others' time. A moment passed cannot be regained.

17.   Be the change you want to see. Let the change start with you. When you start changing, it will have repercussions on your immediate environment.

18. Believe in the power of the spoken word. Your words will guide you and pave a path for you. Think about achieving your goals and talk positively every time.

19. Believe in the power of visualization. If you can see it, you can be it. Think of achieving your goals constantly, and at the end you will achieve your goals.

20. Channel stress to improve your performance. Use deadlines as challenges and you will be able to meet your goals in time.

21. Concentrate on the activities at hand for a better future. Do not let other thoughts bother you when you are performing a task. Give every task your hundred percent, and the result will be in your favor.

22. Consider yourself a student and not a master. When you consider yourself a student you can keep learning new things. But when you consider yourself a master, your ego doesn't allow you to learn new things.

23. Courage is not the absence of fear but the ability to act in its presence. Pressure and negativity will restrict you from inching closer toward your goal. Be brave and fight hard.

24. Create a strong image of yourself and live up to it. When you create a strong image for yourself, it will motivate you to stay on the righteous path in spite of a few roadblocks.

25. Cultivate a sense of humor. It is often said that laughter is the best medicine. You can learn to laugh at yourself. But do not laugh at others—laugh with others.

26. Dedicate an hour every day for personal development. Engage in any activity, like exercising or meditating, that improves your self-worth.

27. Developing discipline along with dedication will give you results. It will allow you to stay focused and help you concentrate on your goal despite distractions.

28. Do not be a slave of technology. Technology can be both your boon and bane. It can indulge you in unproductive activities or it can take you closer to your goals. Choose wisely.

29. Do not overthink. It will present you with unnecessary options that lead you nowhere. Perform the task once you have decided to do it.

30. Eat the right kind of food. Your body also works on the G.I.G.O. principle of computers. G.I.G.O. stands for "Garbage in, Garbage Out." Your body also reflects what you feed it.

31. Enjoy worldly objects but do not get trapped. Conquer your mind and desires; only then will you be in true control of yourself.

32. Every day before you go to sleep, analyze your day and plan for the next. Notice where you faltered and make efforts to rectify those mistakes.

33. Every opportunity can be viewed as a threat or a challenge. Condition your mind to think about challenges and not threats. People will run away from threats but face and overcome challenges.

34.   Everyone has some strengths and some weaknesses. Concentrate on the strengths of the people and overlook their weaknesses.

35.   Focus on the answer and not on the question. Winners see answers in questions and losers see the questions in every answer. Be a winner and focus on the answers.

36.   Focus on the task and not the peripherals. Do not get lost in the illusion of reward. You can use it to motivate yourself, but dwelling too much on the result can also prompt you to deviate from your task.

37.   Go the extra mile. It is the *extra* that differentiates *extraordinary* from *ordinary*. Push and push hard to remove roadblocks and clear your path. You will achieve your goal easily with a little extra effort.

38.   God has designed you for success and carved a path for you. All you have to do is spot the opportunities and engage yourself to attain your goal. Discover the path and follow the steps to success.

39.   If you waste your time watching television, you cannot get on television. Manage your time well and keep on working toward your goal.

40.   Indulge in an active lifestyle. Sluggishness and laziness will slow you down and resist your development. Active goals will result in an active life.

41.   It is an age-old saying—honesty is the best policy. Be honest with yourself and review your performance regularly. Be true in letting yourself know that you

have failed at a particular task and set at your goal with a vengeance.

42. It is very important stay fit. Without meeting your health goals, you cannot achieve other goals. Choose a program that suits your needs. Staying physically fit will allow you to stay mentally fit as well.

43. Just like you program a computer, you can program your mind as well. Positive thoughts will yield positive results, and negative thoughts will yield negative results.

44. Keep building your willpower. Engage in self-discipline and curb temptations. Think without interruption for a long period of time and you will find answers to your questions.

45 Keep growing. True happiness comes when you achieve your goals. Once you achieve one goal, set another one and another one. There's always scope for improvement.

46. Keep negative thoughts at bay. They will tempt you, but you have to learn to stay away from their alluring call. Once negativity possesses you, it can ruin your life within a few days.

47. Maintaining a diary is a good way of conversing with yourself. It is a dialogue with the subconscious. It has the potential to unlock untapped areas of your mind along with serving as a good storehouse for your memories.

48. Make a habit of reading before going to bed. Take 20 minutes of your time to read every day and you will be amazed with the change this activity brings in you.

49. Make quality decisions and stick to them. You may come across many options, but the important thing is to take decisions and back them up. At every crossing, you will have to make a decision. Spending valuable time making decisions will increase the distance between you and your goals.

50. Manage your time well. Everyone has 24 hours in a day, but the difference between successful and unsuccessful people is how they manage the 24 hours.

51. Nature's law states that efforts will lead to rewards. As you sow, so shall you reap. Your efforts will bear fruit; be sure to protect your dream.

52. Never discount the power of your dreams. Remember, you can get what you want. Believe in your abilities and dare to dream.

53. Nobody is perfect. Perfection is a myth. Making mistakes is a part of life; it can be excused. But making the same mistake again and again cannot be excused. You have to learn from your mistakes and make sure you do not repeat them.

54. Nothing can stop you if you want to pursue your goals. Your willpower will guide you through the darkest phases of your life. Be ready to light the torch and you will find your path.

55. Nothing comes easy in life. There is no free lunch. You have to struggle. Your greatest struggle will become your greatest victory.

56. Notice the tiny things and appreciate simplicity. It will bring clarity to your goals. You will find pleasure in things that others take for granted. By practicing this, you will find yourself beaming with joy even upon witnessing a toddler's smile.

57. Our body grows old, but our mind stays young as long as we want it to be. Do not let physical barriers cripple your thought process. Stay young and energetic in your mind and your body will support you in the pursuit of your goals. It's never too late.

58. Pay now and play later. You have to plant a seed first to enjoy fruits. There is no way you can eat fruit from a tree that has not been planted.

59. People have mastered the art of meditation and practiced it over thousands of years. Spend some quality time with yourself by meditating. Meditation has different forms; praying is also a type of meditation.

60. People who do not have goals will not allow you to succeed. They will laugh at you and try to pull you down, but you have to be resilient.

61. Plan frequently. Keep an hour a week aside to review your progress and make plans for the next week accordingly.

62. Positivity has the power to overcome negativity. A single candle can light many others and conquer darkness.

63. Positivity is contagious. Always stay positive and associate with positive people. People have negative traits, but look out for goodness in people.

64. Push your limits a bit every day, and eventually you will find yourself way ahead of your limitations. Just like increasing the amount of weight while exercising builds muscles, pushing your limits will increase your strengths and better equip you on the pursuit of your goals.

65. Relationships may be made in heaven, but they are strengthened on earth. People are your greatest asset; make sure you value your greatest asset.

66. Remember that diamonds are made under pressure.

67. Replicate what successful people have done. The success formula is the same, you just have to follow it and apply it to your field of work.

68. Rise above hate and treat people the way you want to be treated.

69. Seek mentors and be one when you are ready. The wisdom you gain from your mentor will allow you to reap the benefits of your efforts without committing the mistakes that your mentor had to commit to gain that wisdom.

70. Set aside some time to gain knowledge. Books contain a vast amount of knowledge that has been passed on for generations. Choose your field and learn all there is to know.

71. Share your innate thoughts only with people whom you trust. They will give you the right guidance as they wish well for you. Do not share everything with everyone.

72.   Spend time with likeminded, positive people. If you are a fitness freak, spend time with other fitness freaks. Share your wisdom and learn from their experiences.

73.   Stay close to nature. Plan your trips to places that have abundant natural beauty. Nature has a calming influence on your mind and body. Staying close to it can rejuvenate you so that you can work toward your goal with a renewed zeal.

74.   Take a break. Do not let others control your life. Live your life on your terms and conditions. Taking a break will recharge you and renew your spirit.

75.   Take calculated risks. If you do not take risks, you will not be rewarded. Calculated risks will minimize the prospect of failure and allow you to pursue your goals unhindered.

76.   The day you stop dreaming, you stop changing. When you stop changing, you stagnate and you die. That is the end. Never stop dreaming. Keep moving forward in life; do not stagnate.

77.   The future belongs to those who dream big. Think without limitations and watch your imagination come true. Put a timeline on your dreams to turn them into goals.

78.   The price you pay now is the temporary price for a permanent solution. Your efforts will definitely yield results. You just have to be patient and you will get your reward.

79.	There is a direct connection between your mind and body. Your mind functions at an optimal level when your body is relaxed.

80.	There is an immense amount of power in blessings. Perform unselfish deeds and you will be blessed for life. Try setting and achieving goals that will benefit you as well as others.

81.	Think about what you want in life. Condition your body and mind to work toward your goal. Once you develop a habit of thinking about your goals continuously, your subconscious mind will do it regularly and you will attain your goal.

82.	Think about your legacy. Think about ways you can contribute to the success of your family and the immediate environment.

83.	Think before you speak. Many people speak first and then think about it. Always stay true to your word and fulfil your promises.

84.	Time management will allow you to do things that you want to do. You will be able to achieve a balance between things that you have to do and things you want to do.

85.	 Treat people with respect and ensure that you are also treated with respect. No one has the right to insult you. Stand up once or lie down forever.

86.	Trust the power of submission. Submit your senses to your goal and witness the magic. When you submit yourself to your goal, you will automatically spot opportunities that will lead you there.

87. Trust your life partner and maintain a healthy relationship. Talking with your spouse about matters that bother you is therapeutic.

88. Understand your body language. Your body language communicates a lot more than your words. Exude positivity by following good body language principles.

89. We are a tiny speck compared to the vast universe. Acknowledge this fact and don't let your ego make your decisions. Stay humble and grounded.

90. We are surrounded by noise. Everywhere there is a mobile ringing, music playing, cars honking, someone yelling, etc. Visit a place that offers silence to reflect or review your goals. It can be a religious place or a place closer to nature. Silence is golden.

91. Wear clothes that reflect a strong personality. Certain colors are associated with certain characteristics. Choose your colors wisely and dress accordingly for the event.

92. When you are down and out, the only option you have is to get up. Every adversity has a seed of equal or greater success in it. You have to believe in yourself to achieve greatness.

93. When you go beyond the call of duty to make an effort, you are bound to be blessed. You will have people rooting for you and that positivity will definitely yield results.

94. When you have a dream, you need to nurture it. Do not let anyone take away your dream from you. Consider your goal to be your prized possession.

95. Work like a company. Every company has a mission and a vision statement. They perform S.W.O.T. analyses and make strategies to reach their goals. You should do that for your goals.

96. Work persistently and consistently. If you want a life with recurring rewards then you have to work continuously. If you make an effort just once, you will be successful just once.

97. Write down five things that you would like to achieve if time and money were not a constraint. This is your dream; this is what you truly want.

98. You have the choice to be great. If you think that you are born to be great and set realistic goals, you will invariably get there.

99. You spend most of your time at work and your home. Decorate these places with positive signage. They will condition your mind to stay happy.

100. Your goal will make a huge difference in your life. A life without a goal is liked a parked car—it lacks mobility. Set a goal, take charge, and drive the car toward it.